D1210461

PRAISE FOR
The Glorious Deception:
The Double Life of William Robinson, aka Chung Ling Soo,
the "Marvelous Chinese Conjurer"

"Mr. Steinmeyer's book is like his illusions: a presentation of the seemingly simple in a progression which leads to delight."
—David Mamet

"A lush new biography . . . When [Steinmeyer] describes the performances of Chung Ling Soo, you simultaneously thrill to them from the best seat in the house and watch the trap doors work from underneath the stage. . . . *The Glorious Deception* is a true detective story and a sparkling cultural history."
—Teller

"Captivating . . . In Steinmeyer's capable hands, Robinson becomes a walking, talking illusion and a reminder: never trust appearances when in the presence of a magician."
—*Kirkus Reviews*

"In this affectionate and informed biography, Steinmeyer tantalizingly picks along the trail of the magician's life. . . ."
—*Publishers Weekly*

"Wry and colorful depiction of magical entertainment before and after the turn of the century . . . Steinmeyer has done an awe-inspiring job . . ."
—David Regal, *Genii*

PRAISE FOR
Hiding the Elephant:
How Magicians Invented the Impossible and Learned to Disappear

"Like Mr. Steinmeyer's own magical creations, this book is provocative, entertaining, and original."
—Ricky Jay, author of *Learned Pigs & Fireproof Women*

"Simply the finest, best-told, most graceful history of the Golden Age of magic I've ever read. It belongs on that elite shelf of historical explorations, like *Longitude or The Professor and the Madman*, which are so entertaining, so informative that the reader with no prior interest will feel educated and enthralled on every page."
—Glen David Gold, author of *Carter Beats the Devil*

"A delightful new book. Steinmeyer is a modern master. He writes with wit."
—Michael Pakenham, *Baltimore Sun*

"A wonderful new book. . . . A wonderful history of stage magic and the performers who made it."
—Jon Carroll, *San Francisco Chronicle*

ALSO BY JIM STEINMEYER

The Complete Jarrett

Two Lectures on Theatrical Illusion

The Magic of Alan Wakeling

*Hiding the Elephant: How Magicians Invented the
Impossible and Learned to Disappear*

*The Glorious Deception: The Double Life of
William Robinson, aka Chung Ling Soo, the
"Marvelous Chinese Conjurer"*

The Conjuring Anthology

Art &
Artifice

and other
Essays on Illusion

Concerning the Inventors, Traditions,
Evolution & Rediscovery of Stage Magic

With Twenty-Three Diagrams

Jim Steinmeyer

Foreword by Neil Gaiman

THE CARROLL & GRAF MAGIC LIBRARY
CARROLL & GRAF PUBLISHERS
NEW YORK

ART & ARTIFICE
and Other Essays on Illusion

Carroll & Graf Publishers
An Imprint of Avalon Publishing Group, Inc.
245 West 17th Street, 11th Floor
New York, NY 10011

AVALON
publishing group incorporated

Library of Congress Cataloging-in-Publication Data is available.

ISBN-13: 978-0-78671-806-1
ISBN-10: 0-7867-1806-4

9 8 7 6 5 4 3 2 1

Printed in the United States of America
Distributed by Publishers Group West

FOR HARRY, JAY, JOHN & ALAN:
Who taught me about magic

Foreword:
The Aesthetics of Invention

Over a decade ago, I found myself invited to a "retreat," at which several great minds in their respective fields—futurologists, cyberneticists, musicians, and such—and, inexplicably, me were gathered together to discuss the future, imagine the way things would change in the years ahead. We got some stuff right and lots of things wrong. One of the other people there was Jules Fisher, who really is one of the top people in his field, that of theatrical lighting, and also a former and occasional magician, and we wound up talking about magic and theater. Some months later, out of the blue, he sent me a copy of *Art & Artifice* in its original limited print-run form, and I am still grateful.

There is a magic to illusion. It's the magic you get sitting in the audience watching the girl (or the donkey) vanish or fly, from watching someone walk through a wall or produce a hatful of coins from the air. Your disbelief is suspended, the natural order of things is changed, the world is, for a moment, reimagined. And that thrill is too easily punctured by explanation—someone who has just seen, and been awed by, a miracle will feel cheated and cheapened by seeing it revealed as a trick, part optical illusion, part sliding panel, part bald-faced lie. It's why magicians guard their secrets, why they get huffy and upset when anyone reveals anything; they don't want the explanation to take the magic away.

But there is another magic, equally as valid, and it's the awe of understanding how something was done. The sheer giddy delight at mechanics, at the way that human intellect and imagination can be employed to dupe or trick or befuddle an audience, the intersection of science and showmanship and the power of the imagination. The way that cliché "They do it with mirrors" barely begins to cover what someone like Charles Morritt actually did. It's the point where "How it was done" becomes, not the secret of magic, but part of a different language entirely. And nobody describes that ingenuity, the delight of putting it together combined with the aesthetics of invention, better than Jim Steinmeyer.

Penn and Teller have a sequence called Liftoff For Love, where Teller is put into a cabinet, the cabinet is broken into sections and moved across the stage, the head section is placed down on the ground and opened to reveal Teller's head still inside, and it's then replaced and reassembled. (It's the sort of illusion that used to turn up in magic acts on children's TV when I was a boy, and I'd watch it because there wasn't anything else on, certain only that what seemed to be happening wasn't.) Then they do it all again, this time with a transparent set, and you watch Teller shooting through trapdoors, scooting back and forth beneath the stage, popping his head up once again, like a man in a maniacal ballet, and the trick becomes utterly magical—the energy, the deviousness, the work that goes into the illusion is more impressive than the illusion itself.

This book is like that.

This book of essays is not a book for people who want to know How It Was Done, as much as it is a book for those who want to know Why Anyone Would Want to Do It In The First Place. It's a book about the joy of the chase. This is Jim Steinmeyer at his best, on the trail of a long-forgotten illusion, the secret of which an Edwardian Magician took to his grave, figuring one clue out from the writings of someone who looked without seeing or wrote without thinking; deciphering another clue from half-an-anecdote in a book of reminiscences; taking his knowledge of the history and technology of magic; and then making the process of the illusion, the back-stage stuff with half-bricks and pipes and gaffer tape, become even more magical than the illusion itself.

With his *Hiding the Elephant* Steinmeyer took the public on a journey through the history of theatrical magic. *Art & Artifice* is a backstage tour; it's the perfect book for those who appreciate detective work and the thrill of the chase, those of us who are excited by the description of Devant's Mascot Moth or Morritt's Donkey and wish we could have been there in the old days to marvel and exult and to wonder how the hell it was done. The descriptions are clear, the mysteries excellently unraveled. Steinmeyer's combination of enthusiasm and erudition is a joy.

Every now and again my copy of *Art & Artifice*, the one Jules Fisher gave me, has disappeared, which means that several times in the last decade I've discovered how very near to impossible it is to get a new copy. (Each time I'd given up, my original copy surfaced again. I have stopped wondering where it goes when it's not on my shelves. I probably wouldn't like the answer.) It's one of many reasons that I'm delighted *Art & Artifice* is being republished for a wider audience. Enjoy.

—Neil Gaiman
May, 2006

Preface

These five essays represent the sorts of subjects that most interest me. Even among magicians, the science of stage illusions is often reduced to technical points and secrets. This is to the detriment of our understanding, as the great illusions were integrally products of the times, the traditions and fashions, and the incredible, inventive personalities who brought them to the stage. As we look back, these illusions leave us with mysteries, present us with the human, expedient necessities encountered by any pioneers, and ultimately give us insight into the timeless appeal of magic.

It surprises me, in retrospect, that the strict subjects of these essays center around five individuals and span barely thirty years. Still, these subjects are touchstones to many decades of magic history and ingenuity, and scores of talented performers. The approaches to magic discussed in the essays continue to be inspirations to me and serve as wonderful reminders as to why there is indeed a continuing art to the presentation of illusions on the stage.

—Jim Steinmeyer
Burbank, California
November, 1998

Acknowledgments

I've concluded each essay with notes which include sources, additional references and comments. In addition, my friend, the late T.A. Waters, made insightful editorial notes on the manuscript. I'm especially grateful to my wife Frankie Glass, for her careful reading and important advice throughout.

Contents

1. Art & Artifice

> I remember as a boy seeing Sir Henry Irving's
> production of Faust, and being greatly impressed
> by his awesome Brocken scene and then, a few
> nights afterwards, being taken behind the scenes
> at the same theatre. I remember the awful shock
> of disillusion I got when I saw the labyrinth of
> canvas scenery and ropes, and the men in
> shirtsleeves working lights.
>
> —David Devant

Magicians guard an empty safe. There are few secrets that they possess which are beyond a gradeschool science class, little technology more complex than a rubber band, a square of black fabric or a length of thread.

There are no real principles worthy of being cherished, only crude expediencies. But magicians have learned to appreciate how such simple devices can be manipulated into illusion, how a piece of thread can, through feints and contrivances, form the centerpiece for five minutes of entertainment. The art of the magician is not found in the simple deception, but in what surrounds it, the construction of a reality which supports the illusion.

Archimedes said of the lever, "Give me a place to stand and I'll move the earth." The challenge, of course, was in finding the place to stand. When it comes to magic, we can discuss the lever used—devices and sleights—or the movement of the earth—the effect caused on the audience. But first the master magician concerns himself with the soil. He takes his stance, locks his knees, digs in his heels, then begins to gently push—establishing the necessary reality, then levering it into magic. The proportion of reality to illusion has long been the purview of the theatre, and the dilemma faced by wizards of the stage.

•

The story of Steele MacKaye is one of the most unusual in the American theatre. A century has demonstrated that he is most conveniently ignored, an embarrassment to his theatre contemporaries and held responsible, the day after his death, for "the greatest failure in the theatrical world." Yet it is impossible to separate the tragic story of his own life from the artifice of the stage.

In many ways he was the archetype of the 19th century producer—which made the embarrassment acute. Henry Irving, Edwin Booth, Dion Boucicault, Augustin Daly, William Gillette and David Belasco were friends and associates of MacKaye, separated from his affectations and schemes only by degree. Like these contemporaries, MacKaye proudly based his theatrical work in realism. But such realism was a relative term, and this era of popular theatre consisted of wood and cardboard locomotives which careened from behind the curtains, painted canvas castles which were assailed, creaking motorized treadmills which propelled live horse races on stage. The traditions had begun with Victorian melodrama or pantomime, where spectacle, sensation scenes or transformations were obligatory and competition was fierce. "For a person to bring out a merely talking drama," explained the former manager of the Drury Lane Theatre, "is useless. The people will not go to that theatre; they will go where there is scenic effect and mechanical effects to please the eye." Scenic shipwrecks, balloon flights, train crashes or conflagrations were all greeted with gasps and admiration for their realism—a common compliment for the most contrived flourishes.

The New York critic Nym Crinkle explained MacKaye's mastery:

> As a stage artificer, I believe it will be conceded, sooner or later, that Steele MacKaye has no equal. [The] theatric purpose is to hold the spectators through the senses. You are asked only to look and to vibrate. So with Mr. Henry Irving's productions, color always has precedence of character, and

the lines are arranged to catch the eye before in-
trinsic purpose is thought of. But this is the point:
Mr. Steele MacKaye has outreached with pictorial
art all our importers.

Booth and Belasco were known for their obses-
sive, scholarly detail in setting; Daly and Boucicault
had perfected elaborate scene climaxes with outlandish
effects. MacKaye, the toast of Broadway, actor,
playwright, inventor, manager and teacher, developed a
precise notion of realism from the same intoxicating,
heightened fashions. In turn, his fine sense of illusion on
stage led to the dire melodrama of his life.

He was born James Morrison Steel MacKaye in
1842 at Rochester, New York. Early in his career he
dropped his first names, then adopted the Scottish pro-
nunciation of the family name, so that it rhymed with
"sky." His father was a colonel and took steps to provide his son with a military education. But young James
served only months during the Civil War and his brief
army career included amateur dramatic roles. He
achieved the rank of Major before taking sick leave. In
1869 he visited the aged Parisian speech instructor,
François Delsarte. MacKaye was Delsarte's last great
pupil, and the experience changed his life.

The Delsarte system was a 19th century novelty, based in a psychic, religious understanding of
emotion which was realized in gesture. The result was
an attempt to prescribe emotion as a series of rigid, correct actions. Anguish, surprise, appeal for mercy, blank
amazement could all be reduced to poses and taught as

exercises. Hence, acting in the Delsarte style was a formula of gestures, an equation which could be calculated and translated from the chalkboard to the performer. To an ambitious amateur like MacKaye, the Delsarte system was a revelation, and there is reason to believe that he not only imported Delsarte's principles to the United States, but expanded their scope; Delsarte's focus had been oration and song, but MacKaye added "harmonic gymnastics," which included pantomime.

MacKaye demonstrated on stage with a series of ambitious roles, designed to showcase his sense of reality. In 1872 in New York he enacted the title role of *Monaldi* at the St. James Theatre. As the mad artist, the part called for a dramatic burst of insanity at the climax. One night his fitful acting actually caused him to faint, and the actors on stage discovered, upon giving the proper cue, that he could not be revived.

Another scene in *Monaldi* called for MacKaye to sculpt a clay portrait of the leading actress. For the first two weeks, he actually created a sculpture every night during the scene. Finally, the effort exhausted him, and he resorted to uncovering a portrait which was concealed in a lump of clay. ("Just to think," one critic had recorded a lady's comment after watching Edwin's Booth historic 1870 production of *Hamlet*, "the gravedigger must dig a real grave every night. I never saw more than a shovelful of earth taken up before, but at Booth's he takes up a whole barrelful. It's perfectly splendid.")

MacKaye became the first American to play Hamlet in London, appearing in the Opera House of the Crystal Palace with Tom Taylor's company on May 3, 1873. The *Hamlet* experiment was an attractive one, and the press was fascinated by his "easy and natural attitudes." But the Delsarte system remained a curiosity. Of one later role an American critic commented:

> *He acts by a kind of algebra.... It is only fair to say that he gets there just the same, and with an accuracy that fully bears out the simile.... His acting, in addition to these intelligible strokes, is further distinguished by a profusion of graceful but meaningless gesture and action, very much like a writing master's flourishes.*

"Algebra" was a word which clung to Delsarte, a vague complaint about its mathematical precision. MacKaye was masterful at teaching the Delsarte techniques and could make a dramatic appearance on stage: he was a solid, square-jawed man with flowing black hair and a small mustache. Still, the most reliable accounts suggest that his own roles were self-conscious and mannered. A friend and critic commented that MacKaye "never gave himself to the drudgery of acting with a single purpose; he must be playwright, star and manager."

•

MacKaye's *Hamlet* closed just days before Maskelyne and Cooke, on the other side of London, opened their theatre of magic at Egyptian Hall. The

Hall had, for decades, been the home of curiosities and popular entertainments. It was built in 1811 by Bullock to house his museum; the carved sphinxes, lotus columns and Egyptian goddesses made a flashy contrast to the red brick Georgian buildings which surrounded it in Piccadilly. It had housed Mexican artifacts, paintings, Napoleon's carriage and even Egyptian tombs. Over the years, the first floor great hall had been converted to a theatre which seated over two hundred people. It was a gloomy room, surrounded by a frieze of hieroglyphics and topped with a dome of odd Egyptian motifs. It was a good theatre for magic. Maskelyne and Cooke adventurously risked a three month lease on the hall, starting May 26, 1873.

They had begun as enthusiastic Cheltenham amateurs in 1865, members in a volunteer band who were inspired by a performance of the Davenport Brothers. The Davenports were two Americans who had quickly capitalized on the new religion, Spiritualism. They were both roped inside their Spirit Cabinet, an oversized wooden armoire; in the darkness spirits materialized, playing musical instruments or rapping on the sides of the cabinet. It was a trick. It was the first escape illusion, but it was topical and controversial, as the Davenports did everything to suggest that there were real ghosts on stage with them.

Maskelyne had discerned the deception and, with his friend Cooke, built his own version to demonstrate the secret. This was the beginning of their career, and they quickly evolved an interesting program. The Spirit Cabinet was always a feature for them. Adding several costume changes at the end of the routine, they created a brief sketch entitled *The Lady and the Gorilla.*

Several years later they added an optical illusion, a large cabinet with a concealed mirror, which inspired several additional effects. They then expanded the sketch, added characters and further refined the apparatus. It was renamed *The Mystic Freaks of Gyges* and, by the time they opened at Egyptian Hall, *Will, the Witch and the Watchman.*

The sketch described a sailor captured by two watchmen and confined in the town lock-up, a portable jail cell. A witch intervened, causing the sailor to disappear. A large black gorilla, another seeming act of witchcraft, appeared to torment the watchmen and a butcher. They schemed to lock up the monkey and sell him, but the monkey disappeared from within a sealed trunk. Finally the witch returned and cast the necessary spell. The sailor reappeared; the players sung a final song verse; tableau.

Will, the Witch continued to evolve for a number of years. The surviving scripts, written by Maskelyne's son Nevil, presumably date from the 1880s.

DADDY: *Now look here! You go that way.*
MILES: *I go that way.*
DADDY: *And I'll go this. We'll scour the country.*
MILES: *With soap and sand.*
DADDY: *We'll leave no stone unturned!*
MILES: *I'll turn them all over.*

DADDY: *I'll have her hanged, Miles, as sure as I'm alive.*
MILES: *I'll have her murdered, as sure as I'm dead!...*
JOE: *It's the old witch who's doing it.*
MILES: *That's who it is.*
JOE: *She ought to be drowned.*
MILES: *Yes, in the Thames.*
JOE: *That would poison her, but that wouldn't matter....*

It was hardly sophisticated. The suggestion of witchcraft allowed for surprises, twists and non-sequiturs which, otherwise, were quite nonsensical. The characters were broadly drawn for farce. Cooke played the sailor or the monkey. Maskelyne specialized in the witch or the Glouchester butcher. There is little doubt, *Will, the Witch* was a full-fledged play, and this was a remarkable idea.

The Egyptian Hall formula was a success, featuring conjurers—some of the finest of the generation like Buatier DeKolta, Paul Valadon, Charles Morritt or Martin Chapender—comic songs, recitals, plate spinning or puppets, and a magic play as the final act. *Will, the Witch* was a regular favorite. Others included *Mrs. Daffodil Downey's Seance*, which featured seance effects; *Ursa Major* involved the magical appearance a large bear, Cooke again in a bear costume; *Elixir Vitae* was a comedy involving a quack doctor and a comic decapitation.

The Maskelyne and Cook engagement at Egyptian Hall extended for over thirty years, then decades longer at their new theatre. They became a London institution, a favorite of families and tourists where their matinees and evening shows—"Daily at 3 and 8," the posters proclaimed—established a permanent theatre of illusion.

•

MacKaye wrote a number of plays including *Hazel Kirke*, a popular mixture of melodrama and fashionable restraint (it was credited as the first play without a villain). *Hazel Kirke* ran for hundreds of performances, then decades longer in revivals and tours, America's most successful play for many years. MacKaye had carelessly signed over his share of the profits to the theatre owners.

Paul Kauvar, a heroic romance of the French Revolution, recreated the waves of mobs and included a horrifying tableau of the guillotine. *Money Mad*, a sensational melodrama, included an elaborate scene set at the Chicago river. The author had contrived to isolate the hero on a bridge crossing the water. During the climactic rescue, the bridge yielded to a passing ship, and pivoted out of the way. The hero was swung across the footlights and above the audience. It was this single scene which carried the evening.

MacKaye also managed two Broadway theatres. His Madison Square Theatre became a showplace for technical innovations, including a unique double stage (one stage atop another in a sort of elevator shaft) which could be quickly lowered or raised to create a complete change of scenery. The double stage was impractical and unnecessary; its best effect was at the end of the play, when it was demonstrated, with the curtains opened wide, as a sort of technical encore.

In the dispute over *Hazel Kirke*, MacKaye left the Madison Square and, several years later, founded the Lyceum in New York. Again, this small, elegant theatre boasted a number of technical innovations— including some of the first folding seats and the first all electric lighting, installed in conjunction with Edison— and MacKaye ambitiously established an acting school as part of the enterprise. As before, MacKaye quickly left when his management was questioned and his first play there was a failure.

In 1886 MacKaye produced, with Buffalo Bill Cody, an enormous Wild West spectacle for Madison Square Garden entitled *The Drama of Civilization*. Such pageantry complemented his ideals, but MacKaye's multiplicity of talents and the continual change of focus always worked to confound his efforts. Otis Skinner described MacKaye as "tall, spare, emotional and eloquent...holding forth to some knot of listeners on some theory destined never to be realized, some dream never to become articulate. He was always magnetic and compelling." In fact, he was often highly-strung and nervous, a man whose sincerity was never doubted but who exasperated those around him.

David Belasco, at that time a stage manager on Broadway, worked with MacKaye in the Lyceum office. One day MacKaye insisted on reading him his upcoming play. It was a dull script called _Dakolar_, which ultimately proved to be unsuccessful, but MacKaye's enthusiasm was the showpiece. Belasco recalled:

> _We sat, I remember, at a large table, he at an end of it and I at a right-hand side. He was a highly excitable person and as his reading progressed he became wildly enthusiastic, hitching his chair nearer and nearer to me, with much extravagant gesticulation, so that I was impelled to hitch my chair further and further away from him, till the two of us almost made a complete circuit of the table before the reading was finished! It was a tiresome experience._

By 1890 MacKaye's career was at an impasse. While recognized as a Broadway impresario, he had actually mortgaged any successful projects, then bore the financial losses of every failure. He searched for his next project and characteristically redoubled his dreams. It was his misfortune to find a situation which would encourage the most improbable scheme. Steele MacKaye later wrote:

> _The ends I aimed at were so audacious that I did not dare, for several years, to divulge the nature of my work, even to my most intimate friends, be-lieving the confession of my secret would secure me only rebukes for wasting my energies on impossible_

*dreams. Then it was I perceived that the great oc-
casion of my lifetime, for the possible fruition of my
hopes, was at hand.*

•

Chicago was planning an elaborate World's Fair
for 1893 to commemorate the 400th anniversary of
Columbus' discovery of America. The site of the fair,
on the shores of Lake Michigan, was conceived by Fair
President H.N. Higgenbotham as a grand neo-classical
"White City" of colonnades and temples. It was an
ambitious plan for a city which had, just twenty years
earlier, been leveled by fire. Since then Chicago was
earning the reputation for rough-and-tumble inno-
vation, but the goal of The Columbian Exposition
would be to finally establish the metropolis, in the eyes
of the world, as one of culture and proportion.

In London, searching for work, MacKaye encountered a group of Chicago businessmen who were
planning the Fair. MacKaye flattered them by promising Chicago his one-of-a-kind theatrical experience. He
was typically persuasive, and if his dreams were tinged
by unreality, it could hardly be noticed within the context of designing domed palaces for the marsh of Chicago's Jackson Park. Fair President Higginbotham described his first meeting with MacKaye in Chicago:

*I have many times regretted that I had not con-
cealed a stenographer to record that evening's
conversation. He came to the meeting without any*

contrivance, neither drawing nor writing, and yet with his wonderful gifts he laid before me such a picture as I never before held, and probably never will again, unless on farther shore I am privileged to renew my acquaintance with that wonderful man and ask him to do me the very great favor of repeating the performance. The full force of all his powers was turned upon me as if I were an army to be conquered, as if an audience of thousands had to be convinced...so he carried me away with him into the clouds. I sat like one entranced, or completely hypnotized, wondering if a sane man could really conduct such a sublime performance.

He had described no mere playhouse. MacKaye imagined a gigantic theatre which would tell the story of Columbus' discovery of the new world. In scale and purpose it was so different that he renamed it Spectatorium to give a sense of the production. He planned to recreate the ocean with a real tank of water; a storm would be whipped up with real waves, wind and mist. The stars over the Atlantic, the sunset of the Azores, the mornings over LaRabida would all be accurately and beautifully recreated. Finally he would portray the ocean crossing with real ships, full-sized crews, rainbows, auroras, meteors and swirling clouds. He would track the approaching coastlines by sliding the foreground and background at different speeds, creating the illusion of perfect perspective.

It is surprising how literal were the effects of the Spectatorium, how in this one startling step MacKaye's artifice was confused with reality. MacKaye would have no painted scenery, only sculptural buildings, islands and ships. His sun was envisioned as a huge, gigantic electrical light, tracking overhead on the precise arc of the sun, then passing behind a veil of tinted glass to create the proper sunset hues. There would be no canvas waves, but real swells on a miniature ocean of real water. His clouds would be projected against a gigantic clear sky. His stars were accurately arranged to portray the skies over the equator.

The Spectatorium would accommodate an audience of 12,000, with a proscenium fully 70 feet tall and 150 feet wide. The stage, an enormous semicircular area, was designed with twenty-five sliding platforms on tracks, which could be pulled from sight, revealing the ocean. This allowed the Nina, Pinta and Santa Maria, built in three-quarter scale, to actually track through the water.

All was subservient to MacKaye's realistic effects, and the scale redefined the nature of stage entertainment. At the Spectatorium, an actor could not be heard. Instead, the performances would be in pantomime. A full orchestra and three concealed choruses would provide the dramatic accompaniment. Accompanying titles would be displayed in scrolling frames at the sides of the stage. As the front proscenium could not effectively be covered with a curtain, MacKaye had devised a curtain of light—a dazzling frame which could, by turning a switch, obscure the audience's view as the scenery was changed.

A company was quickly capitalized with MacKaye as "Director General," and a location was assigned. The Spectatorium would be an independent concession on prime real estate at the north edge of the property. Unlike other pavilions at the fair, which were constructed as wood and steel warehouses with white plaster decorations, the Spectatorium would be a permanent structure of stone, a theatrical temple for the residents of Chicago. MacKaye filed his patents—"The Mighty Twelve," he called them, the dozen inventions which would define the Spectatorium—and he began work on an immense model to demonstrate his effects.

For the libretto of the Columbus story, *The World Finder*, MacKaye turned to his seventeen year old son. Percy MacKaye, who went on to become an important American playwright and poet, idolized his father and was particularly susceptible to his persuasions. Many years later Percy recalled the afternoon when the muse was carefully summoned by MacKaye.

> *In an immense high-ceilinged room overlooking Union Square about six stories up...a hired typewriter was busily typing the scenario while my father sat with Henry Watterson and myself, at a great table piled with manuscripts, charts and building plans. Before long, my father rose from his chair. Oblivious of the clicking machine, he began then to describe to me the physical and spiritual adventures of Christopher Columbus in midocean...till soon the floor of our steam-heated*

hotel room became the gale-swept deck of a
medieval ship where, through the autumnal light
above Union Square, vistas of colossal billows,
looming like wild mountains in motion, were
overhung and shot through with lightning visions
of saints and demons.

Long before he had ceased speaking, the clicking
typewriter had stopped and our room was
breathless with the imagined awe of his recital.

"Now Percy," he said abruptly, "express all that
in a poem for music. Write me the Storm Choral
for my Spectatorio—the typewriter is ready to
copy it." Then he handed me a scratch-pad, led
me to the door of an inner sleeping room, opened
it, pointed in, and said, "Go in there! Don't come
out till you've finished it. Rap on the door when
it's done and I'll let you out, but not before.
Remember, my boy! Knock, and it shall be
opened!"

So, with a mysterious smile, he closed the door
behind me, turning the key in the lock.

In the small, dark bedroom Percy paced, stared
at the paper, and heard rhymes which "hovered and
hummed like bees." After a long period, the words
came to him, which were transferred slowly to the pad.

Go back! Go back!
Ye mad, in ocean's chasms lost...
Trust not the seeming might of waves. Beware!

*Beneath their bulk lies Satan's hollow snare. Go
back!
Here lie the phantom realms where nothing
sleeps,
Where through the scum of slimy ocean grass,
A monstrous hand draws seamen down to deeps,
Where dead of ages toss in rotten mass....*

He knocked, the door opened and his father
excitedly snatched the pages, giving them a matchless
reading. "The pleasure of pleasing *him* was an honor
beyond price," Percy recalled.

•

The building of MacKaye's Spectatorium proceeded for many months, but delays prevented it from
being opened with the fair. The structure was larger
than most on the grounds, and it loomed over the
north end of the Exposition. Photographers tried to
avoid it, but it figured in a number of pictures of the
fair, an immense, hulking construction wrapped in dark
wooden scaffolding. By May 1893, when the first
crowds were welcomed through the gates of The
Columbian Exposition, MacKaye had been busy planning a monthly publication, *The MacKaye Spectatorium
Magazine*, organizing a dramatic school which would
train actors for his production, and sending assistants to
the Caribbean to record the native vegetation. MacKaye
may have underestimated the importance of opening
the project in a timely manner. He knew that the

building was planned as a permanent structure, but every day without receipts from the fair endangered the business plan.

MacKaye made a great show of changing the name of the project from The MacKaye Spectatorium to The Chicago Spectatorium, eager to attract new investors. General Benjamin Butterworth, a fair Commissioner and a partner in the Spectatorium, was shocked by MacKaye's priorities, writing with concern that friends had warned him not to get into business with the impresario. The opening was announced for July, but by June, MacKaye sensed the worst and quickly turned his attention to an exhibit of the model to reawaken interest in his theatre.

The New York *Dramatic Mirror* reported that the project was in trouble, having absorbed all the available money and stalled. Contractors placed liens on the building. MacKaye scrambled for additional funds, petitioned the business leaders, the newspapers and fair organizers for support, but the empty, half-completed building was declared a fire hazard. It was claimed that $850,000 had gone into the structure, but in July, when the Building Commissioner ordered it removed, it was sold as scrap for just $2,250.

In September, MacKaye hastily sent for his sons so that they could see the fair. Together, they toured the magnificent grounds, and on the last day of their visit he escorted them to the dark shell of the Spectatorium, through the debris and scaffolding to an iron stairway. They climbed to the top of the structure and looked over the beautiful White City. "Boys, this is where it was to have been," he said simply. A short time later, the half-completed Spectatorium was razed. The demolition took considerable effort; the masonry walls were, in places, twelve feet thick.

Newspapers reported that MacKaye had spent irresponsibly and stockholders had withdrawn their support. Percy disagreed, claiming that the building was victim of the unsteady stock market of 1893 and that investors' plans—roofgardens and restaurants—had greedily expanded the project beyond the original scope. A good amount of graft and corruption plagued the construction, then a momentary bank panic froze the finances and doomed his father's theatre.

However, the failure of the Spectatorium was far more complicated. The case dragged through the Illinois courts for nearly a decade in an effort to assign liabilities. Finally, the Appellate Court of Illinois found the stockholders responsible for all debts. At the center of the company was "a fraud upon all such persons who might thereafter become creditors of such company." MacKaye had traded himself two million dollars in stock, in exchange for the rights to the twelve patents and the script for the show. However, at the time of this transaction, the patents were not filed and the script not written. It was a "trade made by MacKaye with himself and for the sole benefit of himself and his two co-promoters," according to the court. In the sub-sequent years the court attempted to sell the rights to the patents; of course, as they described inventions pe-culiar to the Spectatorium, they were worthless. There was even doubt as to whether the patents, which were inspiring in small models, could have been enlarged to the enormous scale of his theatre.

Percy's 1927 biography of his father was an exhaustive defense of his genius. Among other elements of the story, Percy claimed that Anton Dvorák's potential involvement with the Spectatorium led directly to Dvorák's "New World Symphony;" that Steele MacKaye's suggestions about the building's design to William LeBaron Jenny led to that architect's first skyscrapers several years later; that his lighting innovations were taken up wholesale by the theatre and motion picture industry.

However, Percy's account is filled with such overstatements, and the claims for Jenny or Dvorák are improbable. Dvorák may have been briefly considered for the job of writing music for the Spectatorium, but there is no record of him ever meeting MacKaye, and not the smallest suggestion of MacKaye's vision of Columbus in the "New World Symphony." The claims for theatrical lighting demand a bit more attention. While MacKaye was an early experimenter with electric light on stage, his heavy-handed effects in the Spectatorium have found no equivalents in the modern theatre. MacKaye sought reality through the use of one lamp imitating the sun, a tinted cylinder imitating sunset. It seems that only a single one of MacKaye's twelve patents, which he called the "nebulator," has a modern equivalent in the theatre. This was a rotating cylinder to produce cloud shadows.

In contrast, his associate David Belasco pioneered the modern approach to lighting. By 1900

Belasco had demonstrated his artistry with the famous nighttime vigil in his one-act play *Madame Butterfly*. Standing at the window, waiting for Pinkerton's return, Butterfly was stoic and motionless as the sun slowly set, the stars emerged, the moonlight illuminated the room. Gradually the sky glowed, the sun rose and birds were heard. Still, she waited in silence. The transition, by reliable accounts, was a full fourteen minutes on the stage, and the audience was held breathless watching nothing but the subtle changes of light. Belasco's effects used the same devices which have become standard in the theatre: dimmers, overhead lighting, colored gels on rollers, and backlit scenery.

•

Ironically, Steele MacKaye's project ended as nothing but simple artifice, a sort of peep show. As the Spectatorium company stalled, MacKaye was sick and overworked, but he appealed to financiers and raised $50,000 to vindicate his plans. George Pullman, who had invested heavily in the original Spectatorium project, was happy to contribute additional money for the new scheme. MacKaye rented a former cyclorama on Michigan Avenue and renamed it the Scenitorium. There he built all his effects in large model form, with a stage twelve feet high and twenty feet across.

An offstage chorus and orchestra provided the music, but there was no longer the pretense of actors or theatre. The ailing MacKaye was carried to a podium at the side of the stage. Once 220-pounds, a proud defender of his art, he was now just 130 pounds, so frail that his appearance shocked the audience. Only upon taking controls of the electrical apparatus and reading the libretto did his voice become clear and strong. The glimmer of a night sky, the increasing waves of an ocean voyage, the sliding continents and the rocking ships: for two-and-a-half hours *The World Finder* was enacted in miniature.

Here was the wizard in his laboratory. Here were the illusions, plainly defined. In the best tradition of a magic show, here was the build-up, the climax and the bow. Steele MacKaye hoped that the Scenitorium would demonstrate the quality of his ideas, and while a number of reviewers kindly explained the ingenuity of his inventions, the show seemed an elaborate justification, nothing more than a curiosity. The audience "saw no actors, they heard no poet, but they were gorged with scenery and nothing but scenery," the *Chicago Tribune* wrote. "The eye was feasted and the imagination starved."

MacKaye optimistically explained, in a letter to Percy, that receipts had doubled from one night to the next; technically he was right, but only because of the pitifully small attendance. MacKaye's percentage of the first week amounted to slightly less than ten dollars. To his wife he wrote, "the Scenitorium is a complete financial failure."

At the same time, MacKaye was concealing his illness from his family. For months of rehearsals he had lived on milk, apples or soda crackers. Doctors believed that his inability to take food was a sign of his nervous temperament. He explained in letters that he was suffering from "complete nervous exhaustion combined with frightful neuralgia of the stomach."

After a week at the podium, MacKaye was too ill to continue reading the Scenitorium lecture. Without the inventor there was even less interest in the program. A benefit for him was quickly organized at Hooley's Theatre in Chicago, and a thousand dollars raised. But even with this money, MacKaye was unable to pay his hotel bill, which was only accomplished through the kindness of Alexander Herrmann, the magician. Herrmann, the archetype goateed wizard, was then working at the Chicago Opera House. He was greatly respected in the theatre community, and even had a New York theatre named for him; in turn, Herrmann was always generous to those in the profession.

On February 22, 1894, Steele MacKaye was carried from the Richelieu Hotel to the train station in Chicago. A private Sante Fe railroad car had been donated to carry him to the mild, healthy climate of San Diego. His wife, back in New York, had always joked that the family fortunes were either "cheesecloth or ermine," and under different circumstances this may have been a grand exit, a moment demanding ermine.

MacKaye rallied to express his sincere thanks to the friends at the train station: to Herrmann and the press reporters, to Chicago and its businessmen for their long, patient interest in his work. He had, at that moment, failed at everything and could look forward only to an escape, only a raiment of cheesecloth. Three days later, the train was approaching Timpas, Colorado, when he died. He was 51 years old. An autopsy showed stomach cancer.

The impresario was eulogized in Chicago at his Scenitorium on Michigan Avenue, then in New York with his family and theatrical associates. The obituaries were surprisingly stinging, as if every writer felt a need to explain an awareness of MacKaye's shortcomings or separate themselves from his elaborate schemes. *The Chicago Post* wrote, "He walked with his head always in the clouds; he was perpetually stumbling over petty obstacles that a man with half his genius and twice his practicalness would have made the stepping stones to higher things." His story, according to the *Chicago Tribune*, was "pitiable and pathetic," an actor and inventor "to whom all was real that appeared so unreal to others."

With the Spectatorium, MacKaye had fashioned his lever; the production of *The World Finder* endeavored to move the earth. But to find his footing, he had to completely manufacture the place to stand. His Spectatorium needed to redefine a theatrical production—the actors, the acting style, the story and storytelling, the music, the size, shape and sound. Ultimately the Spectatorium could have been built and the theatrical apparatus could have operated, but MacKaye's artistic foundation was never in place. The failure of the Spectatorium was a failure of the ground beneath his feet.

•

By the end of 1893, David Devant was the new star in magic. He had been born David Wighton in 1868 in London, educated for the profession by Professor Hoffmann's books and apprenticed leaning against the counters at Frank Hiam's magic shop in Nile Street. He once noticed a painting in a gallery with the French title, "David devant Goliath," (David in front of Goliath) and thought it suggested an attractive name for a performer. Devant had quickly mastered the varied and necessary skills of a society entertainer: hand shadows, sleight-of-hand, paper folding, the pudding in the hat. He was solidly built, with a mop of curly hair, a small mustache and toothy smile. Some time around 1883, he discovered Egyptian Hall and began attending regularly, taking in the innovative performances, secretly plotting to appear on that stage.

It took ten years. In August 1893 Charles Morritt left the Maskelynes' employ and Devant, appearing at the Crystal Palace, appealed to the stoic John Nevil Maskelyne for an engagement. His hand shadows and elegant conjuring were skillful, but his ingenuity had been clearly displayed in the audition for Maskelyne. Devant had created a large framework cabinet which he called Vice Versa, in which a man changed into a woman.

Maskelyne was interested, but pointed out that the apparatus was too cumbersome for the tiny Egyptian Hall stage. Devant returned five days later with a small model of a new illusion, a creative adaptation of Vice Versa. He suggested an artist's studio in which the picture came to life.

This memorable illusion fitted precisely with Maskelyne's vision of the Egyptian Hall shows. It was arranged as a sketch, unusually dramatic and serious for Maskelyne. *The Artist's Dream* was simple story of a beleaguered artist who painted a portrait of his deceased wife.

> *MAURICE: Another restless night has passed, and all*
> *That makes night welcome to the wearied soul—*
> *The blessed boon of dark forgetfulness,*
> *Sleep, the sweet parent of a world of dreams*
> *Where pleasure reigns supreme—these are all fled,*
> *And thro' the slow, sad hours, my fevered eyes*
> *Stare, in mute anguish, at the cold blank wall.*

Maurice slept, and in his dream the spirit of his wife emerged from the painting. The blank verse accompaniment, which now seems starched and uncomfortable, was provided by Mel B. Spurr, a popular entertainer at the Hall, and enacted by the Maskelyne company. Devant himself was credited as the inventor, but did not appear in *The Artist's Dream* until years later, when he presented a pantomime version in the music halls.

Devant was made a permanent member of the company in February of 1894. He distinguished himself with his magic, by producing and showing some of the first moving pictures in London, and managing the successful touring company of Maskelyne and Cook.

Occasionally he took a role in a play, like *Trapped by Magic*, which featured a levitation illusion.

John Nevil Maskelyne remained the impresario of Egyptian Hall. His son later calculated that *Will, the Witch and the Watchman* had been performed, in revivals and touring companies, over eleven thousand times. In 1904, when Maskelyne lost the lease on Egyptian Hall, he planned a move to St. George's Hall in Langham Place. This was an austere, undistinguished theatre in the shadow of All Soul's church off Regent Street. It accommodated more people than the auditorium at Egyptian Hall, and Maskelyne used the opportunity to dramatically change his programs. No longer would he present conjuring shows, but would present full plays in which his special effects were integrated into the story. It was the logical step for a master magician, and a tempting ideal after thirty years of success as a producer.

Maskelyne knew that his competition, the West End theatres, had been filled with spectacle and sensation. Henry Irving or Henry Beerbohm Tree—the celebrated actor-managers—had continued the Victorian trend of crowd-pleasing effects to ensure that Goethe or Shakespeare were box office successes. Yet these effects, the Maskelyne family knew very well, were often simply large, coarse stage illusions.

For example, in 1902, three years before the move to St. George's Hall, London was thrilled by a revival of Irving's sensational production of *Faust* at the Lyceum. It was an evening of supernatural thrills. Irving himself took the role of Mephistopheles. The famous

Brocken scene, pure spectacle added to Goethe's script, included hundreds of witches and goblins cavorting on a blasted mountaintop, then flying overhead. Irving included peals of thunder, flashes of lightning, mist and moonlight. For the sword duel, Maskelyne had been consulted at Irving's request, and supplied Mephistopheles with electrical rapiers which sparked and hummed with a surreal blue flame.

The following year saw Tree's *Richard II,* which delighted his audience with a procession of horses and a mob of people onstage. Such spectacle continued with his production of *The Tempest,* which began with a dramatic shipwreck and continued with a number of romantic tableaux of the enchanted island.

Meanwhile, other London theatres like the Adelphi, the Hippodrome and Drury Lane offered a regular diet of spectacular effects. Often enough the shows were written around the devices themselves, just as a magician might arrange his script around an invention. On the Drury Lane stage submarines sailed, horses raced, trains collided, giants marched and balloons ascended. In 1902 they imported the American play *Ben Hur,* featuring a Roman galleon sinking within canvas waves, and the famous chariot race, in which real horses galloped atop treadmills in the stage as rolling scenery completed the illusion.

Typical of the admixtures in popular theatre was the production which opened at the Duke of York's on December 22, 1904. J. M. Barrie's new script, *Peter Pan,* included fantastic scenes of pirate ships, mermaids, and Indian campfires. It was a fairy tale, and through it all, Peter Pan often took to the air. This was accomplished with wires, harnesses and tracks: the flying system provided by the Kirby family.

The Maskelynes announced that their new production at St. George's Hall would open just one week later. They had devised an elaborate show based on Lord Lytton's novel, *The Coming Race*, written by Nevil Maskelyne and David Christie Murray. Lytton's novel was early science fiction, an elaborate Jules Verne-style story of an advanced race of people living beneath the surface of the earth.

The Coming Race demanded a full complement of effects, including an earthquake and falling rocks, a gigantic prehistoric monster, mechanical automatons which glided across the stage, and a number of mysterious levitations—the race beneath the earth controlled a force called "vril" which allowed them to float. The same careful attention which the Maskelynes had brought to their magic shows was now turned to special effects. For example, Peter Pan had flown above the stage on a thick black wire which was visible to the audience. This was in the tradition of decades of "flying ballet" spectacles, which inspired thrills if little mystery. But the Maskelynes had devised their own ingenious system for levitations just several years earlier. A geometric arrangement of fine wires, meticulously balanced and adjusted, could support a person yet remain invisible on a brilliantly lighted stage. This was the secret which would be used to simulate the force of "vril" and float the characters in *The Coming Race*.

Devant recorded that the preparations for *The Coming Race* dragged on; leading actors were engaged for the roles as John Nevil Maskelyne spent lavishly, determined to establish himself as a respected theatrical producer. He planned to present *The Coming Race* twice daily for as long as possible, then continue the play in the evenings, using his conjuring shows for matinees.

"On January 2nd, 1905, St. George's Hall was opened by Mr. Maskelyne with the play he hoped would supersede his former style of entertainment and eclipse all his previous efforts," Devant wrote many years later. Within eight weeks it had closed. Devant himself never saw the play. He was in Edinburgh with the Maskelyne touring company, generating the cash which was being poured into the London production. Devant charitably suggested that the play might have been "over the heads" of the audience, or that the new theatre itself was uninviting. But the more obvious suggestion is that the play was a disappointment. While the audience may have been intrigued by Maskelyne magic, they were disappointed by a series of Maskelyne special effects.

•

In the theatre, a special effect often is designed to be subsumed within the fantasy of the production. To ignore its presence, to fall under the spell and accept an effect without question or wonder is the highest compliment, Coleridge's "willing suspension of disbelief."

An illusion seeks the opposite. It starts with a basic reality and attempts to make it deliberately special or surprising. In a magic show, there is no willing suspension. The magician cannot risk the audience ignoring his illusions or accepting them as part of a larger context; they must be held apart and treated as unique.

If a painting were to fall off your wall you might think it unremarkable. You might wonder if a nail rusted or a wire snapped. You would repair it and forget it the following day. But if a medium were conducting a seance in your home at the precise moment, that painting would change your life. The medium directs your attention, defines the importance of the occurrence and grounds it in a specific reality.

John Nevil Maskelyne had been mistaken in competing with the West End theatres. His product had always been different, and for many years this had been his advantage. Maskelyne's shows had featured a magician—the medium who could quickly and efficiently establish the reality for the audience, then transform artifice into magic. Without this advantage, his product was no better than the collection of fantasy found in any London theatre. There is little doubt that the Maskelyne system of levitation was more amazing than the Kirbys' wire, but Peter Pan's "fairy dust" was much more interesting than "vril." Maskelyne could not compete on that level.

•

The Coming Race was withdrawn and a series of musical concerts occupied the hall as Maskelyne nervously debated his next move. He wired Devant and asked him to bring his conjuring performances to St. George's Hall. Devant suggested a program titled *A Feast of Magic*, featuring his recent successes. Maskelyne pressed Devant to use the costly elements of *The Coming Race* in his magic show, but Devant was firm and "declined to return under these conditions." Eventually the only remains of *The Coming Race* were several small effects which could be included in a sequence of magic called *The Gnome's Grot.*

It was at this point that David Devant, formerly in charge of the touring company, became essential to the success of the Maskelyne theatre. He was offered the managing partnership in the firm. In 1905 it became "Maskelyne and Devant's," a name which was famous through Edwardian London. ("Not that I approve of all these Maskelyne and Devant carryings-on," Noel Coward wrote for Elvira, the ghost, in his 1941 play *Blithe Spirit*.) "I felt a keen sense of responsibility to save the sinking ship," Devant later wrote. "At the same time I had the confidence born of overcoming so many similar difficulties in the provinces, and I knew the power of advertising. Furthermore, I had nearly finished preparing a really good show and new illusions."

In the years that followed, Devant used St. George's Hall as his laboratory, and he continued the tradition of the magic play, creating *The Mascot Moth*,

The Enchanted Hive, *The Magical Master*, *St. Valentine's Eve* and many others. Devant knew his importance to the enterprise. He closed his biography, *My Magic Life*, with an appendix titled "Sketches Produced at the Egyptian Hall during a Period of 32 Years." A list of sixteen sketches followed. Then he listed "Sketches Produced at St. George's Hall from January 1905 to 1915," a title constructed to remind the reader of Devant's precious ten years as managing partner. Here he listed twenty-one titles. So that the point was not missed, the appendix continued: "Illusions and Effects Produced at the Egyptian Hall during a Period of 32 Years," then eighteen titles. "Illusions and Effects Produced at St. George's Hall from January 1905 to 1915," and thirty-eight titles.

Over the years, Devant was also called upon to create illusions for West End shows, including the magic for *Kismet*, for H. B. Irving's *Dr. Jekyll and Mr. Hyde*, and for Arthur Bourchier's and Henry Beerbohm Tree's *Macbeth*. But his head was never turned by such projects. "All these, and sundry other producers, expected me to work miracles," he wrote. "They themselves took months to produce their plays, but expected the illusionary effects to be contrived and made in a few days." His effects weren't completely successful in the hands of actors; Devant complained that they were "not conjurers!"

Devant approached every assignment as a conjurer, and even the plays he devised for St. George's Hall seem to be of a markedly different quality from those by the Maskelynes. They were more restrained, more self-conscious. In an effort to extract the maximum impact from each illusion, they were placed intricately within the play, like a gem in a setting. A number of the sketches built towards one single effect—a sentimental situation which was resolved with an illusion or a spell. Some scripts, quite inelegantly, concerned a magician presenting a magic show. Devant carefully avoided the farce of the early Maskelyne romps like *Will, the Witch and the Watch*, as if suspiciously holding the plot in tight reign. One can easily feel the traditional build-up, climax and bow which would have seemed necessary to a great conjurer like Devant.

"Magical sketches are an excellent means of making one or two illusions go a long way," Devant wrote years later, explaining his philosophy in blunt terms. "They are also very important, or can be made to seem important by atmosphere and setting, thereby greatly enhancing the total effect of the illusion." The play itself was an artifice, and Devant always viewed the theatrical elements and the illusion as very separate things.

•

Devant's approach was the salvation of St. George's Hall. On April 24, 1905, he stepped onto that stage for the first time. He presented The Golliwog Ball (a wooden ball that rolled up a plank), The Crystal Clock (a clock hand that turned without clockwork), Mental Magnetism (mindreading) and other wonders. In The Mystic Kettle he picked up a tin teakettle and stood at the footlights. It was a marked contrast to the prehistoric monsters, the caves, airships and palaces which had recently occupied the same stage.

> *This kettle has a story attached—as well as a handle and spout. When in Edinburgh I was taken to a shebeen. A shebeen in a place where one buys drinks during prohibited hours, but I don't suppose there is such a place in London, unless it is under some other title. The reason I went to the shebeen was not to get a drink; I went there to interview the old gentleman, now passed away, who kept the place. He had the reputation of being a magician. As a souvenir of my visit the old man gave me this tin kettle. The trick he did with the kettle was this. Suppose a person came in to buy a glass of whisky. The old man would pour it out of the kettle as I am doing now. Is there any gentleman here who happens to know the taste of whiskey? A gentleman over there looks rather like it. Now, supposing a policeman, or any other total abstainer came in and asked the proprietor what he kept in that kettle, he would pour out a glass of cold, white, wet water, as I do now.*

A collection of tiny lies, in words and deeds, are stacked and arranged ingeniously to form the battlement for an illusion. David Thompson called it "the dainty torture of a magic show, the small talk that traps." There is no theatrical leap or fantasy, no suspension of disbelief, none of MacKaye's or Irving's heightened realities. So the conjurer remains immune from the fashions of the West End or Broadway, untouched by the palpable advances of technology and science.

Devant himself admitted that his history for the kettle was entirely imaginary, but he delivered it "with an air of great sincerity." In that moment he was the medium at the seance, looking his subjects squarely in the eye, taking their hands, comforting them in a darkened room, resolutely singing his hymn of sincerity, weaving a false reality in the most innocent manner. Then the illusions could begin. From his kettle he would pour whisky, then water. He followed with a small glass of sweetened gin, then claret, Benedictine, port, Chartreuse and milk, Devant's feet planted firmly at St. George's Hall.

Notes

Magicians may have already encountered Steele MacKaye's name in Hopkins' book, *Magic*, 1897, where on page 271 his elevator stage is described and illustrated. In fact, MacKaye is only briefly mentioned in theatrical histories. I was first made aware of his story in written accounts of the 1893 Chicago World's Fair. As the story of the Spectatorium was an embarrassment to him and to the city, even in this context it seldom occupies more than a footnote. The best source for material on his life is his son Percy's 1927 biography, titled *Epoch (The Life of Steele MacKaye, Genius of the Theatre, In Relation to His Times & Contemporaries)*, published by Boni & Liveright.

Previous accounts have relied on Percy's book and have missed important elements of the story, including the controversies surrounding MacKaye's death and the failure of the Spectatorium, which appear here for the first time. *Epoch* presents a number of problems. It is an enormous memoir, bound in two volumes totaling over one-thousand pages. Percy filled the books with tedious footnotes, repetitive references, endless claims and endorsements. *Epoch* has overwhelmed and dominated any subsequent analyses of MacKaye, but Percy's book includes elaborate overstatements about his father's work. For example, the swinging bridge in MacKaye's melodrama *Money Mad* was described by him as:

> *...the first practicable moving stage above the audi-*
> *ence...probably for the first time in the modern theatre,*
> *an elevated, aerial, horizontal plane of the auditorium*
> *was utilized for dramatic action in conjunction with ac-*
> *tion of the stage proper. Not until the first production of*
> *Reinhardt's "Sumurun" was the New York theatre*
> *again to witness the use of the audience plane...."*

Actually, *Money Mad* was, according to critics, a "crude, noisy melodrama," which offered one good gimmick: the swinging bridge. It started no revolution in the theatre.

I had the opportunity to visit the MacKaye family collection at the Dartmouth University special collections, which include Steele MacKaye's correspondence on the Spectatorium, scrapbooks, and scripts. It is easy to speculate about the psychology behind Percy's glorification of his father. Percy, at eighteen, must have been devastated by his father's death. But he must have been equally shocked at the revelations which followed. Obituaries revealed that MacKaye had been traveling west with an actress named Helen Marr, who MacKaye identified to the press as "Mrs. MacKaye." In fact, the real Mrs. MacKaye was waiting dutifully at the family's Shirley, Massachusetts cottage or with a relative in New York City. *Epoch* made no mention of this. Percy portrayed his father as a devoted husband and father, a loving inspiration to the family. The extensive files at Dartmouth pointedly have no family correspondence around the time of Steele MacKaye's death.

Even more disappointing to Percy, the obituaries must have revealed his father's troubled reputation within the theatre community. *Epoch* portrayed him as admired by all his contemporaries and honored for his innovations. But *The New York Times* front page obituary, published the day after Steele MacKaye's death, was wilting. *The Times* savagely criticized his career as an actor, playwright and theatre manager, then painfully placed the blame for the Spectatorium squarely on his shoulders:

> *As a manager and director he was several times very conspicuous and very loud in his proclamations of great reforms, but, though capital responded to his call and men of wealth succumbed to his magnetism, he has left no monument in our theatres....* [The Spectatorium was] *about half completed when the stockholders became alarmed at MacKaye's prodigious expenditure of money. MacKaye tried in vain to get the men whom he had led along so far to follow him to the end. But they could be fooled no longer. Even to their unpracticed eyes, his schemed appeared so chimerical, when they were partly brought to the light of day, as to make them certain that they had engaged in an enterprise which was doomed to be the greatest failure in the theatrical world. ...It would surely have proved a financial failure even if it had been an artistic triumph.*

In my brief description of MacKaye's career, I've tried to balance the accounts. *Epoch* has complete information on his plays and inventions, as well as the story of the Spectatorium. I've also used information from MacKaye letters and scrapbooks, contemporary New York and

Chicago newspapers, *The Northeastern Reporter*, January 3, 1908, and the *Appellate Court of Illinois Abstract of Record*, Term 263, October, 1905. MacKaye is recalled in William Winter's *The Life of David Belasco*, 1918; *The Memories of Rose Eytinge*, 1905; and Otis Skinner's *Footlights and Spotlights*, 1923. Among modern sources were Gerald Bordman's *American Theatre, A Chronicle of Comedy and Drama, 1869-1914*, 1994; and A. Nicholas Vardac's *Stage to Screen*, 1949, which also recounts MacKaye's reviews and innovations.

There are very few sources on François Delsarte's system. The late Orson Welles once described it to me by saying, "The bad acting in silent films...they think they're doing Delsarte," which seems to leave nothing to the imagination. The best book is Ted Shawn's *Every Little Movement (A Book about Delsarte)*, 1954.

The works of other producers and tradition of spectacle melodramas are described in Percy Fitzgerald's *The World Behind the Scenes*, 1881, Charles Shattuck's *The Hamlet of Edwin Booth*, 1969; Craig Timberlake's *The Bishop of Broadway*, 1954; Lise-Lone Marker's *David Belasco, Naturalism in the American Theatre*, 1975; Michael R. Booth's *Victorian Spectacular Theatre, 1850-1910*, 1981; and Dennis Castle's *Sensation Smith of Drury Lane*, 1984.

I have used Devant's books, *My Magic Life*, 1931 and *Secrets of My Magic*, 1936, for the story of his part with the Maskelyne theatres. His appendix in *My Magic Life* includes the script for *The Artist's Dream*. *Secrets of My Magic* recounts the presentation for The Enchanted Kettle. Other sources included George A. Jenness' *Maskelyne and Cooke, Egyptian Hall London, 1873-1904*, 1967 and Sam Sharpe's books *Devant's Delightful Delusions*, 1990, and *The Magic Play*, 1976, which includes the text of *Will, the Witch and the Watch*. Ann and John Davenport kindly

shared their research for her upcoming collaboration with
John Salisse, a history of Maskelyne and Devant at St.
George's Hall. This included a list of the magic plays pro-
duced by the Maskelynes and information on *The Coming
Race*. The latter play was also described in the *Magic
Circular*, December 1964 and May 1965.

My discussions of the role of a magician and his
secrets is based, in part, from my own 1997 lecture
"Reminding and Deceiving." David Thompson's quote is
from *Rosebud, The Story of Orson Welles*, 1996.

Finally, I restaged a version of *The Artist's Dream*
for Jonathan and Charlotte Pendragon for Thames
Television; the illusion was revised to suit their style and
the plot told at a modern pace, but this version, almost a
century after Devant's invention, proved the soundness of
his conception. In November of 1997 I had an opportunity
to reconstruct the first Maskelyne magic play, *Will, the
Witch and the Watch,* for the Fifth Los Angeles Conference
on Magic History, together with the other Conference
organizers, Mike Caveney, John Gaughan, and Joan
Lawton. We purged the text of some Victorianisms and
tightened the script, but were true to the characters,
situations and the sequence of illusions. *Will, the Witch* was
a revelation, a nearly perfect combination of magic and
story. The plot was clear, the characters amusing, and the illusions neatly highlighted. Our talented cast consisted of
John Carney, Jim Piper, Patrick Albanese, Don Bice,
Lesley Lange and Craig Dickens. I described the production in the December 1997 issue of *MAGIC* Magazine.

2. The Moth in the Spotlight

One night my wife saw me get up, light a candle at the bedside and sit watching the flame intently for some time. I then blew the candle out and got back to bed. In the morning I told her that I had a wonderful dream. I had dreamt I was chasing a moth about the stage, a moth who was a human being with wings, and was trying to tempt it towards me with the candle flame when it suddenly shriveled up and disappeared.

David Devant interpreted the vision as a problem, then solved it. Translated to the stage as The Mascot Moth, his sudden and surprising disappearance of a lady, it reached an amazing apotheosis in the art of stage magic. When it premiered on August 7, 1905 at St. George's Hall, the Maskelyne and Devant theatre in Langham Place, the result was some paradigm of understanding—the transcendent mixture of perception and mechanics. It might be the finest evidence of Devant's mastery. Ninety years later it is still an inspiration and a dangerous temptation, just as the original flame tempted the moth.

The first achievement was how closely the dream was replicated.

Originally The Mascot Moth was presented, in the fashion of St. George's Hall, as the climactic illusion in a one act play of the same name. The first script, written by H.L. Adams, was an odd and dark story, in which the disappearance of the moth brought good news in the form of the death of a romantic rival, an entomologist. Within six months the surrounding drama had been rewritten by Devant. The new story included more conjuring, was lighter and traded on more innocent situations. Devant starred as the ill-fated Bob Wentworth. Set in a romantic outpost in the Empire, Rajpoor, India, a group of Britons passed the time with various amusements. The men were engaged in a high-stakes poker game, off-stage, which grew perilous as Bob, betrothed to the beautiful Maude, obsessively gambled money for his marriage. Meanwhile the ladies were entertained by Munga, an Indian juggler and his troupe, who presented several illusions including a levitation and the materialization of flowers and fruit.

As the conjuring performance climaxed, so did the off-stage game. Bob had been ruined, losing not only his bankroll but any hopes of marriage. The conjurer promised to save his best trick for last, the Mascot

Moth. The Moth "comes only once in twenty years. When it comes, it is luck!" Munga announced.

Bob was distracted and intrigued by the mystery. From a dark alcove the fakir revealed the Moth, a lady in a voluminous winged costume hovering above the stage. Slowly she descended, stepped forward, paused center stage and closed the wings around her face.

Bob circled, curious at the apparition. "But where does the luck come in?" he asked. "You touch him, sahib, touch him," Munga urged.

Approaching tentatively, Bob stepped to the shrouded figure and moved his body against her as if to envelop her in his arms. Just as he reached out, there was a momentary flash of movement. In a split second the Moth seemed to disappear up and to an indeterminate spot in space—as if a flame burst and were suddenly inhaled into the air.

Bob's surprise was broken as another poker player entered to announce that his fortune was saved. They had discovered a swindler at the table and recovered all the money. Bob and Maude embraced as the curtain closed.

A particular intrigue of the illusion was the sudden, almost subliminal vision which constituted the lady's disappearance. In fact, she did appear to be swallowed into mid-air, an achievement which became all the clearer, in imagination, when the full secret was explained in Devant's *Secrets of My Magic*.

I had the happy thought of bringing a tube up through the stage [vertically] behind the person to be vanished, who would be wearing a special dress. This dress was made in such a way that it could be supported by the tube and looked the same whether she was in it or not. In the first place it all hung from the neck and the collar, or yolk, was formed by a steel spring shape. Attached to this was a rubber covered reel which, in turn, was attached to a plug of wood snugly fitted into the tube. The reel had some strong cord wound on it, and lay in a pocket at the back of the dress. In one of my various journeys to the lady I picked out this reel and dropped it down the tube which was behind her, then I fitted the plug into the tube, she having folded her wings across her face and locked them together by a steel wire which ran through the top of each wing and hooked them together. Now the weight of the dress was entirely on the tube, the lady gave three taps with her toe and a small bracket lift would glide gently downward [taking her with it]. While this was going on, one of the assistants had looped the cord from the reel over two pulley blocks, one in the floor and one in the ceiling above his head, so that he could get a strong, quick pull on it. The lift having been fastened off, the man who had controlled it stood by the lift underneath the stage. The man with the cord now pulled on the dress and pulled it right through the tube. The moment it was through the man holding the tube let it drop into his hand. The aperture [in the stage] was covered with a small spring flap.

Devant's three-hundred and ten words constitute our full knowledge of this illusion, the best account of its effect and secret. That description, too, accounts for the lingering interest. The Mascot Moth would be another forgotten illusion, a historical curiosity, were it not for Devant's terse insight into its working. Curiously, it does not intrigue from first person accounts on the other side of the footlights—there are precious few reviews and the sudden disappearance, woven tightly within the drama, may have caught observers off guard.

Our regard for the Moth is not that of the critics; instead we read the libretto and admire the author, with the clear perspective that only time can provide.

•

"When it comes, it is luck!"

Mr. Maskelyne, who was never one to shy from a mechanical challenge, told his partner that the Moth was the "trickiest trick he had ever seen." Devant thought it "the best I have ever done."

As always with Devant, whose philosophy and insights were so clear and accessible, the evolution of the Moth is deceptive in its poetry. The story of the wizard's dream disguises the story of the conjurer's careful, evolutionary craft.

The Moth was the end point of an evolution.

Buatier DeKolta's Vanishing Lady premiered in 1886. It is hard to remember that, while ladies had technically disappeared before that date, the notion of this classic effect originated with his modest chair, shawl and newspaper illusion; such was its impact in 1886 and for decades afterwards. DeKolta's effect may be the first "modern" illusion; the frantic interest it created, the headlines, cartoons, "licensed" presenters and imitators it spawned presaged the era of illusion magic which would follow some forty years later. Like Selbit's 1921 Sawing, DeKolta's feature was copied to the extent that it completely exhausted its audience.

In effect, DeKolta spread a newspaper on the stage (to eliminate the suggestion of trap doors), and placed a simple wooden dining chair atop it. A lady was seated in the chair, facing the audience. A large silk shawl was thrown over her; the nature of the fabric allowed her shape to be seen beneath it. Standing behind her, DeKolta pinned the cloth back and adjusted it to clearly show the outlines of her head, shoulders and knees. With a sudden movement he threw his hands open and the lady and cloth disappeared simultaneously, leaving the empty chair. This was shown to the audience, giving no clue to her whereabouts.

Often the lady was seen once again; in DeKolta's case she stepped out from the wings to take her bow and satisfy the apprehensions of the audience.

The chair was not innocent, but elegantly prepared with the addition of a hinged seat which allowed the lady to pass through the stage trap and a corresponding trap in the newspaper. Wire forms attached to the back or sides of the chair could, under the cloth, be pivoted atop the lady to simulate her head, shoulders and knees, concealing her movement through the chair and trap. At the moment of her disappearance, the forms were quickly withdrawn and safely hidden behind the chair again.

Under the auspices of DeKolta, the trick was presented by Charles Bertram at Egyptian Hall in London as the inventor himself made his way to America. From there The Vanishing Lady was copied again and again. A common omission was the disappearance of the veil, performers merely pulling it away to show that the lady was gone. Professor Hoffmann, after carefully writing how the thin silk sheet was snatched up DeKolta's sleeve as he threw his arms open, concluded:

> If all goes well, the effect is extremely magical, the visible disappearance of the veil enhancing the marvel of the invisible disappearance of the lady. Both for the ingenuity of its contrivance and for the personal address evinced in its performance, the trick deserves all praise. But it does not always go well. I have seen it "hang fire" even in the most skillful hands, and I have been assured by performers who have made it a part of their programme that they never approached this portion of the feat without the dread of failure. The whole illusion, indeed, is one that demands the minutest finish [and] there is risk of failure at every point, but in none so much as the disappear-

ance of the veil; and even if this is seen (as has now and then been the case) dangling half and half out of the performer's sleeve, adieu to the magic of the illusion. In my own opinion, the additional effect of success is not sufficient to counterbalance the risk of its failure, and this element of the feat is best omitted.

The Professor's advice was hardly necessary at the time it was written, just four years after the premiere of the illusion. Bertram himself had omitted the vanish of the fabric, as did almost every performer after DeKolta.

•

Devant's Moth might be seen as a logical, more efficient (in theory if not practice) and purer (in concept if not machinery) extension of DeKolta's original Vanishing Lady. But it was not merely an improvement or an inevitable development. The Mascot Moth brought a new understanding and a new sensibility to stage illusions.

Ingeniously, Devant's support—the tube—was the vehicle for the disappearance, the keystone to the entire mystery. While DeKolta had succeeded in the use of natural properties like a chair and silk shawl, Devant bested him by using no visible apparatus. The necessary wire forms were not insinuated atop the lady, DeKolta's expedience, but were incorporated into her moth-like wardrobe. Those wire forms and the fabric costume, then the tube support itself, were all pulled away in separate but virtually instantaneous steps.

Magicians have become numb to the persistent and mistaken notion that "the hand is quicker than the eye." Such imperceptible speed isn't possible with deft fingers, let alone a large silk costume. Some magicians have lamented this; Devant profited from it. The rapid movement of DeKolta's shawl, which could so assuredly ruin the illusion as its destination was perceived, became an asset with the Moth. That movement, up and into some location four feet in space, was an integral part of its effect.

By nature it was no longer a mere illusion. There was no place for the inevitable preparation of DeKolta's effect—the newspaper, the chair, the shawl, the performer standing tentatively behind her as if to begin the countdown or announce his "voilà." Devant had succeeded in subverting many of the essential presentational points, a leapfrog of an experiment which had curious results.

As the magician was not mechanically minded, the construction fell to Henry Bate. In his book of secrets, Devant had an amusing account of how a local constable stumbled into the first rehearsals of the Moth; he was drawn to a window by Devant's on-cue screams. It seems that a significant part of the story, however, is that Bate built the apparatus and installed it in his own photo studio in Brighton. Devant, busy with performances, saw it only after it was completed and ready to rehearse.

Of course, the delicacies of performance were quickly addressed by Devant. As he wrote:

> *My part of it was to get my left foot in front of the tube [that is, between the tube and the figure of the lady], which was facilitated by two stops let into the boards, so that I could get into the right position when I wanted to work the "vanish." The cord was pulled on my giving a shout. Immediately afterwards the tube was drawn down and the process covered by my right foot being brought up sharply with the left, the heel of the left foot going into the side of the right foot. In this position the tube was entirely covered in its passage downwards.*

He approached the lady from her right, with his right side towards the spectators, sliding his left foot behind her (and between her and the tube). The stops would have insured that the tube ended up immediately behind his left heel.

As the costume disappeared up, he swept both feet together by bringing his right leg tightly against his left. This positioned his upright body immediately down-stage of the tube, so that it was hidden during the split second that it dropped through the floor. (One presumes that the tube was black or of a very dark color corresponding to the background. Devant was photographed performing the illusion in his traditional black tails, but during the original play he wore a light color.) Devant could then step away from the spot, clearly showing that the lady was not to be seen.

In later years Devant presented a New Version Mascot Moth at his theatre, which presumably was a simpler variation on the illusion. He had more success when he interpolated the disappearance into several other sketches, using it in *The Magician's Heart* and again in *The Artist's Dream* (a later, pantomime version, presented in Music Halls, of the original Egyptian Hall drama). In both cases, he eliminated the moth wings by having the lady turn her back on the audience.

> *She had golden hair hanging right down her back and she wore a white silk dress à la Galatea. The golden hair was a wig which was attached to a sort of skeleton head-piece made of steel wire and also shoulder-pieces made to fold upward [to pass down the tube, which was] a much bigger one than that for the Mascot Moth. In this case I wore a long cloak which I put round the tube as the dress was making its way down. Most people thought it vanished into my clothes somehow or somewhere, but they couldn't give a satisfactory explanation about the woman, so they were not much nearer the truth.*

As he hinted, the final moment was diminished by the necessary cover of the gown. In *The Magician's Heart* or *The Artist's Dream*, Devant again approached the figure from her right side, but in opening his right, or down-stage, side of the long dressing gown, it must have covered a great deal, to the detriment of the illusion. The Moth tube would, presumably, be some four to five inches in diameter (a substantial Edwardian costume passed through it); _The Artist's Dream_ Tube may have been six inches or larger.

After Devant's retirement _The Artist's Dream_ was toured by Cecil Lyle, using the original apparatus. Devant may have sold a duplicate to Thurston in 1908, but it seems to have never been presented. Kellar and Nicola performed the illusion in their own shows, for brief periods of time, but it was not a popular favorite outside of Devant's repertoire. Ironically, its celebrated simplicity of effect made it virtually unsuitable for a magic show, where tricks are understandably appreciated when they occupy some time on stage, where apparatus in evidence provides a change of scene or color, allowing for presentation and misdirection. The effect of the Moth was a mere split second, best on a bare stage.

Devant correctly diagnosed the perfect element for his Moth, as a part in a dramatic play or pantomime. There the necessary misdirection, during the preparation for the vanish, could be found in the surrounding drama. There the lack of apparatus increased the surprise. As the climactic moment of _The Mascot Moth_, its original drama, or the surprising and unexpected finish of _The Artist's Dream_, the Moth was a fitting mystery.

"It was a difficult thing to get right in rehearsal," Devant concluded his description, and one wonders if this wasn't an understatement. The preparation was difficult for a touring show. The timing, syn-chronized by the performers and stagehands, was very delicate. If the dress disappeared too slowly, or without enough cover from the performer's body, it could seem to be pulled into his costume. If the performer pro-vided too much cover it appeared as if the lady had simply disappeared through a trap.

"The trickiest trick," Mr. Maskelyne had said.

•

I was tempted by the Moth; in 1981 I had enough understanding of illusions to read into his sub-tle effect and enough ignorance to misread the perilous staging which was hinted between the lines. When I was hired by Doug Henning that year to work on the illu-sions for *Merlin*, his upcoming Broadway show, my knowledge of the Moth was part of my magic lexicon.

Merlin was an ambitious project, an expensive Broadway show which would mark Doug's return to New York. From its earliest outlines it was brimming with illusions. Incorporated were several short presenta-tional sequences (as Munga stopped the action to perform for the British, young *Merlin* would stop occa-sionally to demonstrates his powers). The other effects were integrated, if not completely disguised, within the scenery, the stage or costumes. *Merlin* became famous, that season, as a fabulously overstuffed and confused Broadway spectacle. The critics savaged its mixed mes-sages of scenery, music and script. But the magic was uniformly praised and, from deep within the project, the magic was an absolutely glorious experiment in the integration of illusion into a story, made possible only through the success and idealism of Doug Henning.

Not surprisingly, The Mascot Moth had been included from the earliest draft; this would be our opportunity to recreate the mystery. Together with John Gaughan, in charge of diagnosing and developing the appropriate apparatus, we began our homework, inquiring of people who had seen the illusion performed or might have insight into its workings. But there was precious little to discover. We rehashed Devant's three-hundred and ten words, reading them out loud slower and slower, doing our best to act them out or transcribe their meanings into sketches. Overwhelmed with the enormity of the show and fearful of the legendary Moth, I successfully petitioned to have it removed from the show. The illusion seemed far too perilous for a nightly show. Perhaps, I reasoned, we could conquer it if it were staged for a television special—a one-time performance in which all of our attention could be directed to the problem. But as we continued to think about the illusion, it became apparent that the only way to solve it was with the repetition of a stage show. Several months later, with other problems solved and renewed optimism, John and I quietly put it back into the outline, promising Doug that we could replicate Devant's Moth.

The illusion was one of the last completed for *Merlin*, without any opportunity for Doug to rehearse it in Los Angeles. John Gaughan brought a series of sound judgements to the apparatus—new materials, engineered catches and locks—which would have been unavailable in 1912. The end result was an ungainly tower of steel tubing, eight feet tall, containing the necessary traps and tracks. Overhead a sheet of four- by eight-foot plywood, seemingly balanced on top, was the staging area. By climbing a ladder and dodging the overhead beams one could "perform" the illusion in the shop. A mock-up gown, of violet and lavender satin, was snapped in place and then pulled through the tube as we precariously danced Devant's choreography around the tiny, wobbly stage.

From eight feet over the shop floor, the three-hundred and ten word liturgy took on a new meaning. Now the trap moved smoothly; the tube rose, locked in place and fell; the lady could stage her descent and the assistants practice their positions. Each of Devant's words became clear and succinct, down to the smallest suggestions of presentation.

From eight feet over the shop floor, we realized that Devant had withheld nothing; he had written out the complete secret and handed it to us in his modest little book.

The Moth was disassembled and shipped to New York for *Merlin*. At the costumer's, John's sparse wire framework was redressed in a gauzy white silk shroud, giving the lady a wraith-like appearance. The metal tower, along with other heavy pieces of apparatus, was being installed in a new show deck, an elaborate construction which replaced the current stage at the Mark Hellenger theatre and occupied weeks of time.

Downtown, at 890 Broadway, the scene was blocked and staged in a rehearsal space. Debby Henning would stand stationary as the stage manager talked through the action of the scene. Doug, standing to her side, would take a step towards her as she would duck out of the way—representing her miraculous disappearance by a simple, expedient exit.

Sitting in the bleachers, I watched with a certain helplessness. I knew that I could not, with only my brief rehearsals atop the tower, pretend to inform them of the finer points. It would all change when we were with the apparatus on-stage.

Steve Kirsner and Willie Kennedy, Doug's technicians who would be operating the illusion, also watched. Leaning up against the black concrete walls they contemplated the pale, necessary simulation, marking time until we all knew better. As the unseen actors in the Moth, they would ultimately be responsible for her disappearance.

We arranged to sneak onto the stage, with the clandestine blessing of stage management, late one day when rehearsals were over. We bundled the rehearsal costume into a bag, took the subway uptown and met at the stage door. No stars, no directors or producers. I had insisted that we needed a little time, in secret, with the apparatus. Just four of us, just an hour or so, I asked, to anticipate the tasks ahead of us.

Now that the Moth apparatus had been swallowed by the smooth black floor and completely disappeared, the task was even more intimidating. There was no tower, no tiny staging area, no visual "cause" and "effect" to contemplate. Magicians idealize the notion of an illusion without apparatus, but facing such a construction is unsettling and disorienting. The expanse of the floor separated the secret into two worlds. From below was a tangle of steel and wooden platforms. From above there was just a bare stage, and the feeling that we were, once again, back at square one—seemingly nothing—with Devant's Moth.

We ran through the illusion six or eight times in silence, examining the views from the extreme seats, synchronizing the dance under the stage and anticipating the action above it. We identified several problem angles and plotted solutions: a bit of wardrobe, a simple manipulation of the elevator to lead the lady to the trap.

The costume was tucked back into the bag and we stepped out the stage door onto 51st Street. Our thoughts were far from David Devant or Brighton of 1905, but our confidence must have been identical to that of the originator as he first watched his dream Moth, with a shout, dissolve into the air.

•

The Queen schemes to bring down Merlin; she gazes into a crystal ball, attempting to find his weakness. A pool of light comes up center as Merlin and Philomena enter; this scene constitutes the Queen's vision. Merlin is sent to study his books and spells; he crouches on the stage, center, with Philomena, his trusted assistant, to his left. Merlin is still young and easily distracted; soon he is lost in a reverie of knights and castles and adventures. He stands, as if visualizing the fantasy before him. "I'll give my love to a princess in a tower...a great and beautiful lady!"

Philomena looks on disapprovingly, but the Queen, standing down stage center, makes a careful study of Merlin's dream. "True love, of course!" she says to herself, satisfied that she has the key to a plan. Pulling her cape around her, she steps stage right.

Merlin gestures to the side, extending his arm. From the darkness a ghostly vision steps on-stage, a lovely princess in a long, gauze-like white silk dress and cowl. She steps towards Merlin, moving within a cloud of vapor, and pirouettes slowly, as if tempting him with her beauty.

From under the stage, Steve, Willie and Mike Phillips have moved along a small platform to the down-stage Moth trap. There a small lamp is covered with a dark blue gel so as to not throw light up through the stage. Steve stands to the side, at the counterweighted arbor, a hand-over-hand loop of rope which controls the elevator trap. Mike reaches up to hinge open the small square trap, about five inches across, which covers the tube. Willie, on the up-stage side of the trap, places a hand on the black velvet covered tube.

Steve unlocks the trap and eases the pressure off of it. By dropping the elevator trap slightly, about one-half an inch, he gives Debby an opportunity to feel the location of the trap without looking down to find it. Debby, in thin ballet slippers, can feel the edges of the trap, which is only a rectangle of nine by fifteen inches.

The elevator is counterweighted in excess of her weight; still, the trap feels "soft" as Debby moves on it, insuring that she has found the correct spot on stage.

(When the stage carpenters first took the stage and examined the equipment, one stood over the tiny trap and asked, "What goes through that?" "Not what, *who*!" we told him. He sternly warned that putting someone through a trap that size would only break their legs and arms, and threatened that it would be rebuilt inside of a week. By then we were confident in our dimensions. Because the Moth trap served double duty during the show, raising an actor into position in the first act, it needed to be reset before every performance, with the elevator in the lower position. As it was counterweighted, the only efficient way was for someone to "ride it down," providing weight on the trap. Several months into the run, virtually every carpenter had ridden the Moth trap down through the stage floor.)

It requires the careful synchronization of five people to make the Moth disappear. Two are above the stage. Three are beneath the stage. Although they are just inches apart, there is no visual contact and it seemed to me that an audience, who might well suspect the presence of trap doors during a magic show, cannot imagine the intricate coordination without witnessing both teams working together. Willie refers to it as a "great cue," appreciating the combination of a fine touch and self-assurance within no more than a second or two.

Merlin's dream lady pauses center stage, gesturing towards him with her long, wing-like sleeves of white silk. She tosses her arms over her head, covering her face with the sleeves, as Merlin steps behind her, admiringly.

"Now I know what I must do!" the Queen contemplates, crossing down-stage of the vision, from stage right to left.

She continues, recitativo, "It's about romance / It's about daydreams / It's about following one's heart, a popular mistake / It's about now I know *the moves I need to* make!*"*

Placing his hand under the tube, Willie pushes it straight up until the catch locks it in place, about four feet over the stage floor and immediately behind Debby's back. As it rises, a catch at the mouth of the tube contacts a small block at the back of her costume and—quite often—automatically locks it in place. Doug's move around the lady is to ensure that this happens. If the alignment of the block and tube are off, he can give it a slight adjustment as he crosses behind her; it is a gesture as if reaching to place a hand on her shoulder.

Debby throws her hands and sleeves over her face, reaching to the back of a small cap to contact two points of Velcro at her fingertips which will lock the sleeves in place. Because our dream lady is no longer a moth, the sleeves are no longer wing-shaped. They hang softly over her head and shoulders in the clear shape of a person.

As soon as she feels the sleeves in place, Debby slowly slides her arms down, out of the sleeves and back to the sides of her body. The goal is to not betray this movement; it must be done smoothly within the thin costume.

The stage manager, out front, gives a cue through the headset that Debby is covered. Steve pulls smoothly on the arbor ropes, and the elevator lowers. The tiny trap drops quickly, within four or five seconds, taking Debby through the stage floor. The Queen's movements, down-stage of the action, cover any movement. Simultaneously, Doug circles the shrouded figure, watching to ensure that he crosses down-stage as she is moving through the dress. Debby must turn her feet sideways on the small elevator, arch her shoulders in tightly and turn her head, tucking her chin against her chest so that it cannot bump on the edge of the trap opening.

As she is lowered, she must lean back slightly, so that her forehead doesn't brush against the front edge of the dress, betraying the downward sweep of movement.

By the time she leaves the dress, now empty and supported by the tube, Debby is wearing only a smooth body suit. But the back of the dress, a panel of white silk, is attached to it, so that we are able to remove as much of the costume as possible before the vanish. As speed is of the essence, no excessive fabric should be pulled through the tube.

Merlin has crossed up-stage of the lady to the stage left side of her. He glances down at Philomena, who gestures that he should return to his studies.

"You're right, Philomena; I should stop daydreaming."

Debby, still standing on the elevator beneath the stage, continues crouching to be out of the way of the operators. Mike steps in and swings the trap closed over her head, then lifts the thin nozzle of a fog machine to a hole, about the diameter of a fingertip, in the center of the trap. He pumps a small quantity of oil fog through the stage and into the empty dress, so that several seconds later the smoke will accentuate the disappearance.

Steve locks the arbor and steps to the side. Willie moves to the bottom of the tube, where the pull cord for the dress terminates in a rope handle. His other hands contacts a pull cord attached to the tube lock. Holding the handle he stands at the edge of the catwalk, ready for the Stage Manager's cue.

Doug is wearing a thin, light colored shirt and trousers. For this scene he has been given a long, decorative strip of cloth which is worn like a shawl, over this shoulder blades and then hanging straight down from his forearms. This shawl is only ten inches wide, and exactly the length that, when held in front of the tube, it will obscure all of it to the stage floor.

Merlin takes a step towards the lady, lifting his right arm and placing it behind her, the first step towards an embrace.

Standing to the left of the dream lady, Doug slides his right arm behind her—between the empty dress and the tube. In order to do this he grips the shawl gently with his fingertips, pulling it through the space so that it does not bunch up but hangs straight and flat in front of the tube.

Since the Queen's verses, the strings in the orchestra have held the final note in a sustain; there is a tension in its sound, and the promise of an imminent surprise.

"Go Moth," the Stage Manager announces over the headset; that is the cue for the disappearance. Willie pulls straight down as quickly as he can, jumping off the catwalk and crouching as he falls, propelling the dress through the tube overhead. It is pulled over the top of Doug's arm and into the mouth of the tube. Meanwhile the tube is covered by the strip of fabric, hanging straight down, which serves as Doug's shawl. For Willie it is a hard pull; the spring wire shapes in the costume are being quickly squeezed flat. Underneath the stage there is a sudden sound of metal sliding against metal, a dull screech telling the other assistants that the illusion is a success and the dress has reached its destination.

As he reaches the floor, just a fraction of a second after the dress disappeared, Willie pulls the cord which releases the tube. The black velvet-covered tube falls as fast as gravity will take it, landing with a thud on the padded surface beneath it.

Immediately Mike reaches up, swinging closed the small square trap over the tube.

Merlin swings his left arm forward, the gesture of completing his embrace. The lady seems to disappear with a strange flash of movement, up and into his arms as they come together. Simultaneously there is a wisp of smoke remaining on stage, a momentary vapor echoing the position of the dream lady.

Debby is the first out of the steel scaffolding, watching her footing on the small plywood catwalks which form the routes under the stage. Mike follows. Steve checks the lock on the arbor once more before leaving the apparatus.

Merlin brings both arms together, then immediately apart as he takes a step stage left, allowing us to see that the lady has disappeared. In just a moment—a surprising and perplexing moment—the air has swallowed up his vision of a dream lady; the small whirl of vapor at his feet is all that remains. He turns and faces Philomena, who stands obediently at his side. She is not surprised by the vision, she is abashed at Merlin's reverie. The lights fade on the scene; the Queen, watching from down-stage left, has formulated her plan. Merlin will be tempted by a beautiful lady.

Willie straightens up and lifts himself to the catwalk, following the others back up the stairs to the stage.

•

At least three times I have seen such "tricky tricks" approach art, and each time the experience was revelatory. Each belied the cavalier notion that magic is only about the impression taken away by the audience, that method doesn't matter and that technique is a hindrance.

I watched Doug Henning's Things that Go Bump In the Night, (the "Bump Box" we called it) from the edge of the backdrop. I could see the free spirited performance in the bright lights, and the intense, perfect parade of people, animals and machinery, in quiet darkness, which was responsible for the illusion. I marveled at the rehearsals for a levitation: it was a complex assemblage of methods which required, at various times in the routine, five people to be responsible for the lady's journey. There was no way to synchronize the action with music or a headset; each of the five had to take their cues by a sense of touch, from inches away or from across the stage, slowly transferring the illusion, invisibly and as the audience watched, from technician to actor, to technician, then back again.

And, of course, the Moth was another mix of art and technique. It was a "great cue" as Willie said, a challenge of planning and careful execution. The secret was every bit as wonderful as the result on stage, and maybe even more wonderful. There is no shame or irony in that; there is art beyond an ability to make an audience applaud or gasp. It can lie in intangibles and secrets, the synchronization of a cast and crew, the solution to an impossibility, rendered in simple, dependable machinery. These are the profound understandings which can never be explained and which the initiates themselves seldom appreciate.

Notes

DeKolta's illusion has been described in print many times; a neat series of engravings in Hopkins' *Magic*, 1897, shows the illusion exposed. Goldston's *Magician Annual* for 1909-10 has a fine series on the chair, and Peter Warlock's *Buatier DeKolta, Genius of Illusion*, 1993 has a full account of the routine. Professor Hoffmann's description of the workings of the chair, filled with details and subtle touches, appeared as the final effect in *More Magic*, 1890.

Devant's words on his illusion are taken from his *Secrets of My Magic*, 1936. The script for the (second) play of "The Mascot Moth," written by Devant, appeared as an appendix in his biography, *My Magic Life*, 1931. It is interesting to speculate why the play of the *The Mascot Moth* changed so abruptly; the best account of the original Adams play is in *The Wizard* for September 1905. Certainly it was a much darker story and may not have included many of the ancillary conjuring effects which filled out the later script.

Another curiosity is exactly how the disappearance was staged within the final play. Devant's script indicates that the moth suddenly disappears, then the men rush in from the side explaining that they've discovered the cheater and confiscated the money. This is a wonderful dramatic touch and indicates that the dream-like moth is responsible for good fortune. But Ellis Stanyon in *Magic* for July 1906 describes the men rushing in with the good news and Devant's character "having no further use for the moth...announces his intention of making it fly." While this reduces the disappearance to an anti-climax, it is easy to imagine that Devant used the misdirection of the men's entrance to cover the preparations necessary for the illusion.

The Moth was described in the above cited *Magician Annual*, under the name A New Disappearing Lady. It seems a conglomeration of several ideas; the lady has moth wings but turns her back, as in *The Magician's Heart*.

Sam Sharpe, in *Devant's Delightful Delusions*, 1990, discussed the history of the illusion and gave his own recollection of seeing Devant perform it as part of *The Artist's Dream*. Sharpe suggested that the illusion suffered from too much cover provided by Devant's dressing robe.

Will Dexter's colorful book *Secrets of the Conjurer's Craft* (also published as *This is Magic*) contains a chapter on vanishing ladies, including DeKolta's chair and the Moth. He mentioned that Lyle performed the disappearance (in *The Artist's Dream*) by standing between the lady and the tube; the costume disappeared over his shoulder. This sounds odd, in terms of the proportionate space between the objects. Dexter suggests that it was not successful in the illusion it created.

My own file of documents and journals from *Merlin* records the progress of the Moth and the other illusions of the show. By May of 1982 it was finalized in the show and John Gaughan constructed the apparatus within a few months; by August 12 we were able to attempt it in his shop. On November 4 it was in place at the Mark Hellenger, allowing us to sneak in and try it on stage. There Steve Kirsner, Willie Kennedy, and Eileen Molloy

(Debby Henning's stand-in) and I rehearsed the illusion. Glen Priest, Doug's longtime associate, had been responsible for installing the illusion at the theatre.

During the performance, the Moth was presented by Doug Henning as Merlin, Debby Henning as the dream lady, Rebecca Wright as Philomena, and Chita Rivera as the Queen. Mike Phillips assisted with the illusion beneath the stage.

John Gaughan's changes in the machinery, I have no doubt, constituted substantial improvements in the original. The best of these was the nearly automatic lock which connected the "above stage" and "below stage" action at the mouth of the tube. The illusion was surprisingly dependable during the run of the show.

Merlin ran from December 10, 1982 to August 7, 1983 on Broadway. It was produced and directed by Ivan Reitman, written by Richard Levinson and William Link, with music by Elmer Bernstein and lyrics by Don Black. Lines are quoted from the script with permission. For Siegfried and Roy's show at the Mirage Hotel, John Gaughan reconstructed the apparatus; they currently present the illusion with their own surprising and effective staging.

I saw the Moth hundreds of times during the rehearsals and previews of *Merlin*, but once the Moth became the property of its operators, I stayed out front. I am grateful to Willie Kennedy, who operated the illusion in rehearsal and at every performance, and checked my recollections of its machinery and the sequence of moves.

3. Above & Beneath the Saw

Like all else in the world, magic cannot stand still. It must either advance with the times, or fall behind them. And, in this connection, the one quality which above all others is essential to progress is novelty. Without novelty in some form or other, nothing can be achieved in the way of progress. [But magic] inventions are not derived from accidental ideas, happy thoughts, or heaven-born revelations. Their origin is in the fact that inventors are always on the lookout for sources of inspiration, and always endeavoring to imagine novel combinations and novel applications of familiar devices.

Scarcely a decade after he wrote those words, on a grey morning in December of 1920, Nevil Maskelyne's careful logic failed him. With a small group of people, he watched the audition of a new illusion on the stage of St. George's Hall, the Maskelyne theatre. It was a significant new idea, but its importance eluded Maskelyne, and he passed on an option to present it.

Perhaps the dreary, clinical audition deceived him; perhaps he failed to anticipate its drama, or the public interest, or underestimated the abilities of its entrepreneurial creator. Somehow, by Sawing Through a Woman, the British illusionist P.T. Selbit auditioned the perfect product for the decade which would be later said to roar: impulsive, aggressive and thrilling. With it, he made a clean break with the Golden Age mysteries defined by the Maskelynes since the 1870s, and in a logical but significant step, changed the development of stage magic. On that December morning a group of agents from the Moss Empires, watching the same tentative premiere, huddled in a corner of St. George's Hall and decided that Selbit had the new sensation for their theatres.

Sawing Through a Woman was one of magic's few incendiary successes, producing a frantic and colorful chapter in the art, and there is little doubt that magic advanced with the times when Selbit's bold illusion premiered. But seventy-five years later, it is still puzzling to contemplate why. The buzzing activities around the illusion only form the pieces to a puzzle. In retrospect, the Sawing was neither wildly original nor as expertly refined as many contemporary illusions. The interest in the illusion took many by surprise, and professional magicians raced to hold onto, then manage, its success on stage, the way one would saddle an old mare only to discover a bucking bronco. From the perspective of time, there seems a hidden subtext or meaning behind Selbit's fourteen-minute music hall turn. Today we might conclude that for some reason, at that time and place, it was suddenly entertaining to victimize a young lady on the stage.

Selbit, perhaps quite innocently, had come upon the right idea for the right time.

•

Before 1921 it was not a cliché that pretty ladies were teased and tortured by magicians. In the mid-1800s, the innovative French magician Robert-Houdin had used his sons as assistants, a convenience for the magician, but also an advantage for his presentations, as a young boy placed into an uncomfortable setting—crawling atop a table or suspended precariously in the air—would be far more tolerable for his audience. Dr. Lynn's dissection illusion, Morritt's Oh! (a disappearance in a chair), Maskelyne's The Entranced Fakir (the improved levitation), and the Davenport or Maskelyne Spirit Cabinet were all introduced to their theatrical audiences using men as subjects. Victorian proprieties and vestments made it difficult for ladies to be subjects of stage illusions. A notable exception was DeKolta's Vanishing Lady, which called for the subject to seat herself in a dining chair and be covered with a cloth. Obviously, ladies were valued for their decorative and poetic effect—quite naturally they were the subjects of DeKolta's Cocoon, the production of a person as a butterfly, Devant's *Artist's Dream* or Hercat's She, the recreation of the mythic story of a goddess. Increasingly, as a shapely leg was not only acceptable but admired, such trends dictated a cast of slender, attractive beauties. An important consideration, apparent as costumes lost their fullness, was the size and flexibility of the assistants. An illusion built around a lithe woman was considerably more deceptive than one built around a boy or a man.

On an even broader level the theatrical cliché of the threatened woman, the helpless damsel facing a horrible fate, dates only from the 'teens or twenties. The victim tied to the railroad tracks, or strapped to the crosscut saw, are indeed old conventions, first seen on the stage in nineteenth-century melodramas. But when these originated, a man was portrayed as victim; a woman was often the hero. This was no temporary mistake in casting. For fifty years theatrical conventions allowed the woman to be the hero. Then, some time after the turn of the century, in the same years surrounding Selbit's success, the roles were popularly reversed and the modern cliché took hold.

•

The public first witnessed the illusion on January 17, 1921, at the Finsbury Park Empire, north of London. Selbit stepped to the footlights, an elegant performer known for his light touch and deep voice. The subject was matter through matter, he explained, warming up by demonstrating how one small block passed down through a stack of blocks. This apparatus was taken away and Selbit proceeded to the principal mystery at hand.

From the contemporary reviews, an excellent picture of Selbit's presentation can be assembled. The lady was introduced (Jan Glenrose was the lady in rehearsal, Betty Barker was the magician's primary assistant), and a committee of spectators invited onto the stage. To one side was a tall wooden crate of raw wood, "a coffin-like box, only just big enough to contain her," one review noted, making an obvious analogy for Selbit's macabre fantasy. With the volunteers supervising, ropes were tied around the lady's wrists and ankles and neck. The lady backed into the crate. The ropes were passed through corresponding holes in the sides of the box and held taut, on the outside, by the volunteers.

The cabinet lid was closed, the hasps locked, the box lifted and placed across a horizontal stand. The restrained lady knocked and spoke to assure the committee that she was still inside. "A creepy effect is then introduced, the presenter taking a piece of plate glass (about 4 feet by 9 inches wide) and pushing it down through lid and bottom of box without encountering any resistance." This was repeated with two similar sheets of glass, and two sheets of steel, passed horizontally, from front to back through the box. At this point Selbit stopped the dramatic progression to demonstrate how the box had been divided into eight separate sections.

"Now the thrills culminate—to appropriate music the sawing of the box commences." A decided thrill, complementary to the plain unvarnished box and modern, unpretentious presentation, was the physical act of dividing the box in halves. "A business-like cross-cut saw is introduced and two assistants make short work of the box." The saw rasped and roared as it dramatically made its way through the thick pine planks. "Bloodthirsty...hair-raising." It descended, inch by inch, reaching a point where it inevitably reached the lady's body, bound and stretched at full length within the crate; still the assistants proceeded cold-bloodedly. The saw ripped through the bottom board, clattering to the stand beneath, as the magician stepped in to conclude the experiment. "The ropes are cut off close to the box, the plates of glass and metal are removed and, as the affair is pulled asunder there appears the lady none the worse for her ordeal."

Selbit naturally capitalized on his success with publicity stunts. For example, between performances his men poured buckets of murky red liquid into the gutters in front of the theatre, acknowledging the horror which was otherwise suggested on stage. "Perhaps the artistically inclined may affect to scoff at this type of magic, but there was no possibility of doubting that it pleased a large audience at this particular presentation," a review concluded. There were expected comparisons between Selbit's stark torture and the Theatre Grand Guignol. The famous French theatre of terror had opened a company at London's Little Theatre on September 1, 1920. Translated into English for the first time from its rarefied Parisian success, it had startled London audiences. A writer in *The Daily Express* thought that Selbit's new effect could provide a perfect Grand Guignol plot.

*An infuriated husband finds letters addressed to
his wife—they are signed respectively George and
Henry. A saw is taken from the sideboard, [the
wife] is promptly cut in half, and the respective
portions, packed in brown paper parcels, are dis-
patched with best wishes to George and Henry.
This delectable morsel might be sheer joy to the
Little Theatre audiences.*

Although it premiered in 1897 in France, The
Grand Guignol reached an artistic apotheosis, and the
widest public curiosity, as a result of World War I. The
unspeakable carnage which ravaged Europe—over ten
million killed, twenty million wounded—and the
frightening technological advances of warfare had de-
sensitized Europe to all but the most horrific and
grotesque. For the artistic director of The Grand
Guignol, Camile Choise, the War "had introduced a
new realism and horror in life [and] the technology of
death helped enlarge [the] hideous vocabulary of torture: poison gas, explosive devices, electrical cables,
surgical instruments and drills replaced the old pistol,
dagger and primitive sword." The advances in The
Grand Guignol also called for a more refined, varied
acting technique which, in turn, suggested newly insidi-
ous plots and characterizations. Scarcely two years after
the Armistice which ended "The War to End All
Wars," with a generation of young men slaughtered,
the veterans disfigured, shell shocked and burned from
mustard gas, while the "horror in life" was still a vivid

memory, an impresario brought the theatre of terror to the West End.

During the three-year London run, The Grand Guignol was attacked by moralists and censors. Sybil Thorndike, of the respected family of British actors, had been recruited to portray the various victims and demented souls which comprised a typical vaudeville of Grand Guignol playlets. Some plots were farcical, some grotesquely horrific—reveling in exaggerated violence, arch madness, terrifying science and demented sexuality—all interspersed in a teasing formula of "hot and cold showers" today evidenced in the very best roller coasters. There were shocking but never happy endings. Invariably there was bloodletting, according to a cookbook of gruesome secrets, conjuring, trick knives and special effects. Nothing was left to the imagination. The French productions were long infamous for inducing nausea and fainting in its spectators, and the cobblestone alley outside the theatre was often lined with hyperventilating spectators.

By contrast, on Selbit's stage no blood was shed, no unpleasantries exposed within the box, and the magical finale revealed a lady unharmed. Still, the illusionist may have offered his music hall audiences a taste of the controversial theatre which was making headlines in the West End. "One of the strong points in [the illusion's] favour is the absence of all conjurer's apparatus of a conventional nature," a reviewer noted. The modern simplicity of his presentation felt less like conjuring, more like the echo of a maddening, Grand Guignol-like crime in progress.

Another publicity stunt for the Sawing was greeted with delight and offered broader implications of the public's interest. "Congratulations to Selbit on his clever idea and still more clever handling of the publicity side of the production," the Magic Circle's official publication wrote, just days after its premiere. "To offer Christabel Pankhurst £20 a week as a permanent sawing block, that was genius."

Selbit, in jest, had made public offers to Christabel and Sylvia Pankhurst, two leaders of the movement calling for women's voting rights, to be sawn in halves. By the time of his offer, the Pankhursts, with their mother Emmeline, had just completed their part in a notoriously violent and divisive chapter in British history.

From 1905, when the Women's Vote Bill failed in Parliament, the cause of Woman's Suffrage became known for its radical and sensational techniques. Emmeline warned that the goal would require violent means. No longer could the women, or the cause, be thought frivolous. Hunger strikes, arson, bombing and window smashing—blocks and blocks of storefronts at a time, or the prime minister's residence—became established techniques for nearly a decade. In 1907 the suffragettes tussled with police for five hours, with fifty-seven jailed as a result. In 1908 both Emmeline and Christabel were jailed after 100,000 suffragettes stormed Parliament. Emmeline, like many in the cause, made a dizzying routine of her jail sentences. A hunger strike, once inside, granted her release. But according to Britain's newly passed "Cat and Mouse Act," upon regaining her health outside, she was once again jailed to complete her sentence. Emmeline was jailed twelve times in twelve months.

"We are here to claim our rights as women," Christabel said, "not only to be free, but to fight for freedom. It is our privilege, as well as our pride and our joy, to take some part in this militant movement, which, as we believe, means the regeneration of all humanity."

The frightening militance brought the cause attention. However, when the World War was declared and Emmeline Pankhurst urged an end to the protests so that British women could support the war effort, the cause suddenly earned respect. The contributions of all women's work, in factories and homes during the war, were vital. Without the benefit of further riots or hunger strikes the first suffrage bill was passed and, just one month after the Armistice in 1918, British women first won the right to vote.

When Selbit called upon Christabel or Sylvia Pankhurst, he reminded the public of the women who had challenged society by frightening it, faced off with the government, and achieved their goal. The very act of victimizing a lady in 1921 was to victimize the newly enfranchised lady, to remind, with this theatrical revenge, of the previous decade of tumult. As a review concluded, "What a chance for Selbit! To be able to say he has actually 'sawn off' the redoubtable 'Sylvia,' not once, but many times!"

Through the 'teens one European country after another had granted women's voting rights. Suffrage in the America followed a more protracted, less explosive path, but the movement was no less contentious than it had been in Britain. In 1920 the amendment finally passed the requisite number of states and became law. Women received the right to vote in the United States.

By the middle of 1921, the Sawing had made its premiere in New York. Horace Goldin, the American illusionist, claimed—it was the first volley in the Sawing battle—that the idea was his, having appeared to him in a sort of vision in 1906. However, it wasn't until Selbit's success in England that Goldin presented his own version, on June 3, 1921. (Contemporary magicians recorded the obvious: Goldin's idea was developed after hearing of Selbit's success.) That premiere was suspiciously hurried and pointedly public; it was interpolated into the program of the Society of American Magician's Annual Banquet at the McAlpin Hotel in New York, presented grandly to four hundred other magicians to establish a claim. Goldin's autobiography insisted that its success was immediate (but the account is as doubtful as anything one might find in a professional magician's autobiography). More reliable accounts record that it was a curiosity. Even the official report of the banquet, written effusively by Clinton Burgess, managed to omit mention of the trick. After Burgess' account of the program, there was this anonymous addendum:

> *Another act, which deserved special mention, and which followed that of the Floyds, has unfortunately been omitted from the foregoing report. I*

*refer to the new and startling illusion of Horace
Goldin's—that of sawing a man in two! The effect
is as follows: Goldin has one of his assistants recline
himself in a long, shallow box, supported upon a
trestle. The extreme ends of the box are fitted
with sliding doors which may be raised to permit
the hands and feet of the imprisoned assistant to
protrude, and these latter are held by a committee
of two gentlemen from the audience while Goldin,
taking a huge cross-cut saw, similar to those used in
felling a tree, deliberately saws through the box.
The eyes of the audience can follow the saw as it
slowly but surely makes its way down the assistant's body, until all who witness the effect are
certain that the imprisoned man is actually severed
in two. Draw bolts at the central sides of the box
are released and box pulled apart, yet the assistant's hands and feet are still seen protruding and
being held by each volunteer guarding the respective ends of the box. ...The two sections of the box
are finally brought together and the supposedly
bisected assistant revealed none the worse for his
harrowing experience.*

Goldin's first mistake was casting. In hurriedly
arranging his program, he used the services of a hotel
bellboy as victim. He had sawn a man in half, unaware
of the dramatic differences. That mistake was never
repeated.

One magician who recognized the potential of
the illusion was Howard Thurston, attending the ban-

quiet that evening. Thurston entered into an agreement with Goldin: he could present the illusion in his own shows, in return for rebuilding Goldin's apparatus with improvements. It is unclear just how crude, or how nearly complete, was Goldin's original apparatus. The above account, for example, twice mentioned hands and feet protruding from the box, but not the head. (This would have been a notable difference for Goldin's first model. Perhaps the writer simply overlooked this point.) Developed in highly debated proportions by Goldin, Thurston and Dante, the final apparatus did incorporate many deceptive touches drawing from years of illusion; these improvements were not fully reflected in the patent drawings, which were filed by Goldin on September 9, 1921.

Premiered later that year in the Thurston show and on the Keith Vaudeville circuit, this American Sawing achieved the now-famous appearance for the trick. Two decorative chests, side by side, sat atop a heavy table with turned wooden legs. The doors in the chests were opened, displaying the apparatus. The lady reclined inside (Irene Vanderbilt was Goldin's assistant), her head and hands protruding through stocks at one end, her feet through stocks at the other. The chests were closed and a saw used to divide the chests. In this position they were separated, distinctly showing the two halves of the lady.

Goldin's solution to the problem was as much a product of American vaudeville as Selbit's was of Grand Guignol and British music hall. Instead of adorning a plain wooden box with presentation, Goldin's apparatus fit the brightly enameled accouterments of a magician, panels painted with gold *fleurs de lis*, or stenciled Egyptian motifs (as, within the year, it was produced by the Thayer Magic Manufacturing Company). It was purely visual, capable of charming the shortest attention span, and substituted a horrifying suggestion (Sawing Through a Woman) with blatant demonstration (Sawing a Woman in Half). The result was partly amusing, partly surprising.

For Goldin and his audience, there had been no influence from The Grand Guignol, which by 1921, had made no inroads into America. The earliest attempts at staging Grand Guignol scripts concentrated on the mysterious, subtle stories, with little attention from the critics or public. When an authentic troupe of Grand Guignol players opened on Broadway in 1923, the stories were acted in French, and, once again, far tamer than the reputation of the famous theatre. The program ran for seven weeks. It wasn't until 1927 that an American troupe produced Grand Guignol in Greenwich Village with a bill of representative violence and terror. *Time* magazine noted that "there is a great deal of cruelty with a minimum of refinement."

Selbit arrived in New York in September of 1921, quickly taking steps to sue Goldin over the rights to the trick. He failed to stop him, but the British illusionist premiered his own version for the rival Shubert Vaudeville circuit. In a preemptive strike, Goldin had registered most possible titles for the act with the Vaudeville Manager's Protective Association, forcing Selbit to use one neglected title, The Divided Woman.

Variety showed little respect for the originator, and was brutally honest about the differences:

> *Goldin's is called "Sawing a Woman in Half." This one might aptly be titled, "Sawing a Box in Half," for it omits the principal punch of the Goldin presentation, in which the woman's feet and head are seen while the saw apparently passes through her body. ...Selbit lectures the act [and] takes his presentation very seriously, it seems. He bills it as his "baffling, mysterious sensation, direct from Europe, where he created and presented this astounding paradox to the confusion of plagiarists and imitators." These days when most folks refuse to believe in fairies, genii, miracles or their best friends, it is pretty hard to sensationalize American audiences with illusions, [especially] in view of a rival beating Mr. Selbit to it, showing it can be easily duplicated—in fact, there are two Goldin troupes showing it as well if not better.*

Selbit was presenting a chilling "paradox." Goldin, according to his brochure of advance publicity ideas for theatre managers, would never settle for faint praise.

> *Important. Sawing a Woman in Half actually transpires in full view of the audience. They are shown the two separated parts of the woman in plain view. Therefore, please, at no time in your press material, billing, slides or other publicity re-*

fer to it as "An Illusion." By doing so, you merely take away from its sensational value.

Goldin systematized his publicity stunts, having ambulances ready at theatre entrances "in case the saw slips," advertising for carpenters, doctors and surgeons to assist, instigating "challenges" from local women. In short order there were five Goldin troupes, each headed by a different magician (one presented by an actor), fanning out across the Keith circuit to satisfy American audiences. Selbit also instituted his own companies, in America and around the world, to quickly capitalize on the demand. But the inventor was clearly caught off guard by Goldin's head start, and was disgusted at having to scramble to find his market.

The fever for the illusion was soon uncontrollable, and the imitations unmanageable. The Great Leon insisted that he had his own original way of presenting the illusion, and quickly produced it. Linden Heverly, Claude Alexander and David Swift, among others, made claims for the idea. By November, 1921, it was advertised for sale to magicians. The complete apparatus was $175.00, or plans were available in a book for five dollars. Goldin bristled at the copies and, ironically, spent most of his profit dashing to the courts, attempting in vain to enforce his patent.

Goldin suffered from the fact that his illusion was easily and entertainingly exposed with one simple drawing. Many magicians rationalized that the idea was an old one, established in print. For example, the basis of the trick had been explained in one of the most popular books of the era, Hopkins' *Magic*, published in 1897.

> *Another performance of a somewhat similar char-*
> *acter [to the decapitation illusion, just described]*
> *was recently performed at a theatre in New York*
> *in which a clown throws himself on a sofa and is*
> *cut in two by a harlequin. One part of the sofa*
> *with the body remains in one part of the stage*
> *while the other part with the legs and feet (which*
> *are all the time vigorously kicking) disappear*
> *through a wing at the other end of the stage. The*
> *action is very sudden and the effect startling. Of*
> *course, in this case there are two men similarly*
> *dressed. The head and body of one of them ap-*
> *pears at the head end of the sofa, while the body*
> *of the second clown is concealed in the box under*
> *the seat at the other end of the sofa, the feet and*
> *legs alone being exposed.*

Or, from another classic of magic literature, one of Torrini's masterpieces was described by Robert-Houdin in his 1858 *Confidences d'un Prestidigitateur:*

> *At my summons [Torrini related to Robert-*
> *Houdin], two slaves brought in a long and narrow*
> *chest, and a trestle for sawing wood. Antonio*
> *seemed to be terribly alarmed, but I coldly or-*
> *dered the slaves to seize him, place him in the*
> *chest, the cover of which was immediately nailed*
> *down, and lay it across the trestle. Then, taking*

*up the saw, I prepared to cut the chest asunder.
...The chest at length was divided into two parts; I
raised them so that each represented a pedestal; I
then placed them side by side and covered them
with an enormous wicker cone, over which I threw
a large black cloth, on which cabalistic signs were
embroidered in silver. ...A noise was heard, the
cone an the cloth were upset and all the spectators
uttered a cry of surprise and admiration, for two
pages, exactly alike appeared on the pedestals.*

Scarcely a magician lacked these sources on the
bookshelf. Hopkins described a clown divided for
comic effect. Robert-Houdin described a dramatic
presentation of a man sawn into twins. Neither description provided no more than the basic recipe. They
lacked two essential ingredients for Selbit's success: the
climate of 1921, and a lady inside the box.

•

The origins of the popular theatrical spectacles—the victim strapped to the motorized buzz saw or
bound, helpless, across the railroad tracks—have surprising analogies with the Sawing. Not only were such
effects widely imitated and subjects of litigation, but,
like Selbit's illusion, they defined significant clichés.

Today we nostalgically remember that the victim on the buzz saw or the railroad tracks is a Victorian
damsel. But these images began quite differently.
Joseph Arthur's spectacular *Blue Jeans*, one of the last

great melodramas, premiered in New York on October 6, 1890. It boasted a number of extravagant scenes, but the undoubted sensation was the sawmill scene, the first of its kind. With the heroine, June, locked in the office of a sawmill, Perry, the hero, was subdued by the villain, strapped to a moving belt and sent on an inevitable path towards a whirling circular saw. Valiantly, June broke down the door, rushed to the saw and rescued her man at the crucial moment. *Blue Jeans* became a long-running feature of the American stage with the sawmill scene widely copied.

The motorized saw was an admirable novelty (New York audiences, expecting artificial scenery, where thrilled when the saw buzzed menacingly and spit real sawdust), but the dramatic construction of the scene had been well established. Augustin Daly, the influential New York playwright and producer, introduced *Under the Gaslight* on August 12, 1867, a "sensation drama" organized around a series of melodramatic effects, in the style of the day. Daly's most famous invention was the railroad scene.

Laura, the play's heroine, was locked in a signalman's hut for safety while Snorkey, a soldier messenger, went to the nearby railroad tracks to flag a train. The villain entered, overpowered Snorkey, bound him across the rails and exited, leaving the poor man to a certain fate.

> LAURA: *Oh, I must get out.* (Shakes window bars.) *What shall I do?*
> SNORKEY: *Can't you burst the door?*

LAURA: It is locked fast.

SNORKEY: Is there nothing in there? No hammer? No crowbar?

LAURA: Nothing! (Faint whistle in the distance.) *Oh, heavens! The train!* (Paralysed for an instant.) *The axe!*

SNORKEY: Cut the woodwork! Don't mind the lock, cut around it! How my neck tingles. (A blow at the door.) *Courage.* (Another blow.) *Courage!* (The steam whistle is heard again nearer and a rumble on the tracks. Another blow.) *There's a true woman for you! Courage!* (Noise of locomotive with whistle. The door swings open, mutilated, lock hanging, and Laura emerges, axe in hand.) *Here, quick!* (Laura runs and unfastens Snorkey. Headlights glare illuminate the stage.) *Victory! Saved! Hooray!*

The rumble increased as the train approached. Laura pushed Snorkey safely out of the way with only seconds to spare as the locomotive rushed across the stage, from one wing to another. The nail-biting tension and the sensation of the effect, perfectly combined, produced a roar from the audience to match that of the locomotive.

Daly's opening night suffered from nervous accidents. During the climactic moment, the "train" temporarily separated, disclosing the flying legs of its human motor, to hysterical laughter from the audience. However, the artifice of the wood and canvas train was quickly forgiven. *Under the Gaslight* became standard melodramatic fare, running in various productions through the turn of the century. Daly's brother claimed that it had been played "oftener than any other melodrama in the English language."

So successful was it that the famous Dion Boucicault, the master of theatrical sensation, quickly appropriated its famous device for his latest London play, *After Dark,* and constructed a story around it. Here the characters were two men. Gordon Chumley, tied to the tracks, awaited his doom as Tom, locked in a cellar, broke through the stone walls to effect the perilous rescue. Boucicault's play opened in London one year, to the day, after Daly's. When it was produced in the United States Daly brought suit. In the contentious court case, producers pleaded that the effect was not a new idea, that a man tied to the railroad tracks had been included in an earlier magazine story. The final decision centered on the copyright laws—whether the actual stage directions and mechanics could be included in the copyright of the written words. Daly was granted a royalty for each performance of *After Dark.* The ultimate publicity was well worth the price. Bills announcing, "The Great Railroad Scene is Presented" packed the theaters.

Subsequent melodramas explored different combinations, but none, by twentieth-century standards, achieved the proper cliché. For example, in a potboiler named *Saved from the Storm,* a lady was finally bound to the tracks. Here a pack of dogs rushed to her rescue. *The Limited Mail,* opening days after *Blue Jeans,* copied the sawmill scene but placed its daring heroine in danger. Neither of these were lasting successes. For almost fifty years, the man was a suitable victim.

A curious parallel can be found within the script for *Under the Gaslight*. As the train rumbled across the stage and Snorkey was saved by the brave heroine, the final line, indicative of the stilted melodramatic style, was revealing for its emphasis.

> (Laura leans exhausted against the switch.)
> *SNORKEY: And these are the women who ain't to have a vote!*

In 1867 the movement for woman's suffrage was a noble, sincere cause which had taken its first steps towards organization and recognition. By the time voting rights were achieved, in 1920, a great deal had changed. The world had lost its innocence, and crusading ladies had forfeited their innocent charms. Even entertainment had changed—the threat, the hero, the victim—and magicians were in unique positions, dramatizing fantasies, to demonstrate those changes.

●

Selbit attempted to follow the success of the Sawing with a string of other torture illusions. Clearly he was searching for the important imitable quality which would, once again, capture public attention. Destroying a Girl, Growing a Girl, Stretching a Girl, The Indestructible Girl, Crushing a Woman, and

Broadcasting a Woman were produced for his audiences. A number of these effects, along with Selbit's work on The Million Dollar Mystery and The Man Without a Middle, were important, well crafted and deceptive illusions. None achieved the attention of his famous Sawing, which he successfully revived for a 1936 tour.

In 1931 Goldin introduced a significant new version of the Sawing, titled A Living Miracle. The lady was no longer concealed within a box. She reclined on a table as a gigantic, whirling, whining circular saw descended upon her, clearly slicing her in half. The saw was stopped and moved aside, she was lifted from the table and awakened to demonstrate her magical restoration. With the addition of the circular saw, gleaming in the spotlight as it threatened the unprotected damsel, Goldin neatly assembled all of the clichés and emphasized the inevitable terror which may have been missed with his colorful boxes.

When this illusion reached the hands of Harry Blackstone, the popular sawmill melodrama was echoed. A motorized table moved the lady slowly, slowly towards the saw. The magician, wearing a white cowboy hat, watched her fate expectantly, as if helpless. Decades later, the Sawing illusion, by matching the distant inspirations of The Grand Guignol, came full circle: Richiardi's circular saw sliced through the lady, dividing her with a long splatter of blood and a revolting stream of viscera. The audience was invited to not only witness the crime, but to step up on stage and view the body. At the finish, as the last spectators filed off the stage in the funereal procession, Richiardi lifted the victim, groggy and pallid, from the table. The restoration of the lady was perfunctory, a poor resolution carefully offering little relief from the horror. Now the overtones of the illusion were impossible to ignore. When Richiardi presented the illusion in New York in 1971, the theatre was picketed by feminists. Such protests were encouraged by the magician. They provided important publicity for the show.

•

> *In magic, as in all other directions, the chief source from which inventors derive their inspirations is the work already done. But this is where one wants to know where and how to search. ...One must not look at just what is directly in view; one must look all round it, above it, and beyond it. ...One must seek for what may be got out of it, put into it, or suggested by it.*

The twists and turns of the Sawing illusion perfectly illustrated Nevil Maskelyne's words. Funny, frightening, innocent or unwittingly political, the subtle differences defined careers and attracted new audiences. But through the 1920s, the Maskelyne tradition was waning; the days of the cheerful theatre of wonders were passing. After Selbit's illusion proved to be a success in the halls, the Maskelynes staged it in their own theatre. Presented by Captain Clive Maskelyne, it was billed simply as "Matter through Matter," with no mention of ladies or saws. Their title ignored, or denied, the horrific appeal of the illusion which had been unwittingly, delicately assembled atop discomforting issues of society.

"During the past twenty years, magic has suffered a good deal," the hard-boiled magic author Will Goldston wrote in 1933, with the bitter sentimentality of a generation whose ideals had become ignored. Of course he blamed the talking pictures. But the first problem, he wrote, "was the Great War, which turned the world, and people's ideas, topsy-turvy. The demand for entertainment, after the war, was for noise and excitement. Those magicians who were able to adapt their programmes to meet the new condition did well, but they could not re-establish magic in all its old prestige."

Nevil died in 1924, and the sons carried on, suffering from a lack of originality and public interest, battling against trends in popular entertainment. By 1933, St. George's Hall was sold, tellingly, to the BBC for use as a radio studio. During the Christmas season of that year, the last generation of Maskelyne magicians staged a show entitled *Maskelyne's Mysteries*.

Their new home was the Little Theatre, the intimate auditorium which ironically, thirteen years earlier, had hosted the blood and mayhem of The Grand Guignol. There, specialized French illusions had simulated grisly crimes and galvanized London.

Maskelyne's Mysteries offered only perfectly innocent, pleasantly charming illusions. Here was none of the noisy excitement demanded of other entertainments. Oswald Williams presented his routine of tricks from a magic set, surprising a boy from the audience. To comical patter, he spoke of an " 'Orrible Murder," safely illustrated with a handkerchief trick. Noel and Mary Maskelyne produced writing on a slate, performed a series of tricks to accompanying limericks, and concluded with a trunk escape, entitled Chang Foo's Chest.

> *Terminating for the time being—the magic ended at the "Little" on January 20th, 1934—let us hope that London will not be long without this happy show. In these days when so much that is presented as entertainment proves to be something that, to say the least of it, is in questionable taste, may we venture to hope that Maskelynes may long provide that form of amusement which for sixty years has won such well deserved success.*

Even this review from *The Magic Wand*, filled with warm nostalgia and hope, recognized that times had changed. These holiday programs were the Maskelynes' last stand in London, an inauspicious end to their golden, sixty-year tradition.

Notes

This is the first time that the Sawing illusion has been placed into context with social and theatrical trends. I am grateful for the help of Mike Caveney, who has long been interested in the history of the Sawing. When I was preparing the new edition of *Jarrett*, we began swapping information on the subject. He graciously provided me with additional reviews and references for this article.

Nevil Maskelyne's quotations, from *Our Magic*, 1911, is taken from the chapter dealing with Invention. The story of the Sawing has been colorfully related in many histories of magic, most notably Christopher's *Illustrated History of Magic*, 1973. In my own edition of *Jarrett*, 1982 or in *P.T. Selbit, Magical Innovator*, 1989, by Lewis and Warlock, the history and secrets of the routines are discussed. The latter book includes the story of the audition for Maskelyne, which is also discussed in a letter from George Facer to the July/August 1956 *Magic Circular*. Facer, manager of the Maskelyne theatre, was present that morning.

To recount Selbit's premiere, I used quotations from the accounts in the February 1921 *Magic Wand*, the January 1921 *Magician Monthly*, and the February 1921 *Magic Circular*. The latter two include the Pankhurst publicity challenge. *The Magic Wand* issue includes the Grand Guignol reference from *The Daily Express*.

The story of The Grand Guignol is fully recounted in the first English book on the subject, Mel Gordon's *The Grand Guignol, Theatre of Fear and Terror*, 1998. David Skal also includes a chapter on this subject in his exceptional *The Monster Show*, 1993. The accounts of the American versions of Grand Guignol are taken from Leitner, *The Encyclopedia of the New York Stage, 1920-1930*, 1985.

The suffragettes and the crusading Pankhursts are described in numerous histories. My account, including Christabel's quotation, was taken principally from James Trager's *The Women's Chronology*, 1994. The Fourth Franchise Bill, passed in 1917 and instituted in 1918, guaranteed voting rights to women over the age of 30. It wasn't until 1928 that women from the age of 21—like men—were allowed to vote.

Goldin makes his extravagant claims in his autobiography, *It's Fun to be Fooled*, 1937, an aptly named book. Goldin's premise is that, from 1906 to 1921, he couldn't find a producer interested in having the illusion constructed! In frustration, he finally had it built himself in 1921, which is supposed to represent his desperation and diligence, but which hardly seems extreme for an original stage illusionist. Carl Rosini claimed that Goldin got the idea from hearing an account of Selbit's trick (in the 1966 book by Robert Olson, *Carl Rosini, His Life and His Magic*), as did Walter Gibson, in conversations with me. The review of Goldin's first performance (written by Burgess?) is from the July 1921 *Sphinx* magazine.

Thurston relates his involvement with the illusion in his autobiography, *My Life of Magic*, 1929. Dante, according to consensus, suggested adding a bevel to the tabletop, after Servais LeRoy's Asrah, but beyond that his involvement in the illusion's development may have been publicly overstated. Mike Caveney showed me some unpublished materials in which Goldin disagreed with Dante's claim. David Price, in *Magic, A Pictorial History of Conjurers in the Theatre*, 1985, mentioned a Dante souvenir program in his collection with Goldin's annotations complaining of Dante's claims. In The Christopher Collection's *Howard Thurston's Illusion Show Work Book Volume II*, 1992 (annotated by this writer), Thurston's full presentation for the illusion is explained. It involved a large committee on the stage and must have been surprising and humorous.

Goldin's patent, number 1,458,575, was granted June 12, 1923.

The review of Selbit's act is from the September 30, 1921 issue of *Variety*.

As part of his amazing barrage of publicity, Goldin produced a small brochure which detailed stunt after stunt so that theatre managers could capitalize on the effect. A copy of this rare Goldin brochure is in the Jay Marshall collection.

David Bamberg worked with Selbit as part of his American tour. His account is in *Illusion Show*, 1988. Jarrett wrote that Selbit's illusion was very successful in this country. Bamberg disagreed, recording the difficulties in following the Goldin units.

The popularity of the illusion, and ease with which it could be exposed, climaxed in Goldin's unsuccessful court case, 1933 to 1938, against Reynolds Tobacco Company, who had explained the trick in an advertisement. The abstruse Selbit version didn't suffer from the same dilemma, and the illusion was only fully explained—in texts for magicians—within recent years. The Thayer illusion (and Alexander's book, *The Life and Mysteries of the Celebrated Dr. Q*, which had plans for the Sawing) was advertised in the November 1921 *Sphinx*. In the same journal, May 1921, David Swift made his claim. Heverly's plans for his version—a very different effect—are in Mike Caveney's collection. Leon's version is discussed in Caveney's *The Great Leon, Vaudeville Headliner*, 1987. I happen to own Leon's copy of Hopkins' *Magic*. Other than his name and a date carefully inscribed on the fly leaf, the only mark inside the book is found within the paragraph on the Sawing precursor, quoted above. Leon underlined the word "box." The *Magic* account is almost certainly of the Hanlon Brothers, according to Bamberg's book and John McKinven, who is the author of *The Hanlon Brothers*, 1998.

The account of Torrini's Sawing is taken from the Lascelles Wraxall translation of the *Memoirs of Robert-Houdin*. Of course, there has been suspicion as to whether Torrini ever existed, or was simply a creation to enliven the story. Even if the Sawing was not performed, the account was still part of magic literature (as an invention of Robert-Houdin), and the suspicion is that Selbit derived his illusion from this description. Milbourne Christopher (in his notes to the Dover edition of the Memoirs, *King of the Conjurers*, 1964) and Will Dexter (in *Secrets of the Conjurer's Craft*) offer this possibility. It is interesting, and not illogical, to speculate whether the Hopkins account similarly inspired Goldin.

Under the Gaslight, After Dark and Blue Jeans, well established shows of the nineteenth century, are prominent in theatrical histories. My account was drawn from Gerald Bordman's *American Theatre, A Chronicle of Comedy and Drama, 1869-1914*, 1994 (for these and other shows), Joseph Francis Daly's *The Life of Augustin Daly*, 1917 and Richard Fawkes' *Dion Boucicault*, 1979. The play is quoted from Harlowe R. Hoyt's *Town Hall Tonight*, 1955. Kalton C. Lahue's *Bound and Gagged*, 1968 is a history of silent film serials. It is interesting to note that even Pearl White's famous 1914 cliffhanger serial, *The Perils of Pauline*, had not reached the popular cliché. White was known as a courageous daredevil; her characters were seldom helpless victims.

Goldin's Living Miracle was described in Hilliard's *Greater Magic*, 1938.

Goldston's opinions were published in *A Magician's Swan Song*, from the chapter headed "The History of Magic."

The review of the last Maskelyne show, the 1933-34 *Maskelyne's Mysteries*, is from the March-May 1934 *Magic Wand*.

4. Mister Morritt's Donkey (In Theory)

Who would save an ass against his will?

—Horace

The audience had read of it in their programs, anticipating Charles Morritt's latest wonder, The Disappearing Donkey. Now the donkey in question was introduced. Solomon, he was called. Morritt was still, in many ways, the epitome of a magician; tall, elegantly dressed in starched shirtfront, a long square tailcoat and a high stiff collar which, even in

1912, had a faint whiff of nostalgia about it. He was now in his fifties, with an old-world theatricality to his movements which made him intriguing to watch. His co-star was a common, stubborn and wholly disinterested English gray donkey, contemplating the audience beyond the footlights with the perfect mixture of boredom and malice, knowing and innocence. How clever could this creature really be? A genius at its race, Morritt insisted, overflowing with compliments and entreaties which, with a blink, went ignored by Solomon. For the experiment, the donkey was accompanied by a Pierrot clown in full costume: a ruffled collar, satin tunic and white face. This allowed the bland, painted smile to persist as the clown alternately tugged and pushed on his obstinate partner.

The curtain opened on the apparatus, a large, horizontal cabinet standing well away from surrounding scenery. It suggested a small, two-door wooden stable, raised on legs about a foot off the floor.

Two hoops, each roughly three feet in diameter and covered with stretched linen, were brought onto the stage. Morritt suggested that, by surrounding the cabinet with these hoops, it was obvious that the donkey had no route of escape. One hoop was slid underneath the cabinet on the stage floor: the use of a trap door would be impossible. The second was hung from a cord, slightly behind the cabinet: if the donkey exited by

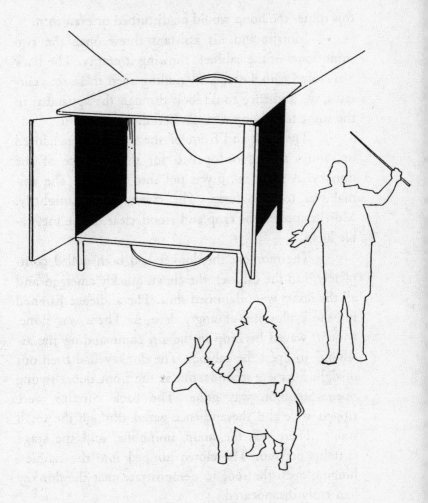

*A reconstruction of Morritt's Disappearing Donkey, based on
contemporary descriptions.*

this route, the hoop would be disturbed or even torn.

Morritt and his assistant threw open the two front doors of the cabinet, showing it empty. The back was closed with a drape. By pulling open these rear curtains, the audience could look through the apparatus to the suspended hoop and the backdrop beyond it.

The back and front of the cabinet were closed up, and a side door opened for the entrance of the donkey. A short ramp was put into position. The animal was true to form. The clown pulled mightily. Morritt applied the crop and stood clear of the inevitable kicks.

The moment the donkey had been pulled completely into the cabinet, the clown quickly emerged and all the doors were slammed shut. The audience listened for the explosions of angry hooves. There was none. Morritt waved his crop in the air, commanding the assistants to open the cabinet. The donkey had been out of sight for mere seconds, but as the front doors swung open, Solomon was gone. The back curtains were ripped aside and the audience gazed through the small stable. There was the hoop, immobile, and the stage curtains beyond. The clown jumped into the cabinet, hinging open the roof to demonstrate that the donkey had truly disappeared.

This is a mystery story. First, it is certainly a mystery about how Solomon disappeared, and the portentous way this secret could be lost. There are also a series of nested mysteries within Charles Morritt's 1912 turn at St. George's Hall. One of those is Morritt himself, a popular British magician whose schemes and indulgences bounced him from the heights to the depths of variety entertainment.

•

The donkey illusion, however, was not the only embarrassing, lost secret in magic. We don't know how Houdini made an elephant disappear. In 1979, when I started work on a new edition of *Jarrett Magic*, Guy Jarrett's very personal book on his creations in stage magic, I found myself sent off in dozens of different directions. It was an attempt to bolster Jarrett's abbreviated text with the full stories of classic illusions and performers. Deep within Jarrett's book was a chapter on the Vanishing Elephant. It was, in many ways, vintage Jarrett, inspired by a chip on his shoulder.

> *Burnside, in the last few years he was producer at the Hippodrome, was all burnt out. He could give birth to no more ideas, and the Hipp shows got no better fast. I wrote to him saying, "Startle press and public alike by vanishing an elephant." I got an answer right back and I went over with a 4-foot stage model, using a derby hat for the bull elephant, and fooled him. He wanted me to leave the model with him, and shot the old crap.*
> *Well, Jack Dane and Clyde Powers had warned me that Burnside would lift anything, from a roll of toilet paper up. But, of course, anyway one doesn't leave models anywhere unless you believe in Santa Claus.*

Burnside decided to pursue another elaborate idea, so Jarrett's trick was rejected.

There are so many people that would rather steal a thing and even make a bum of it, rather than pay for it. They just have that feeling in them. So, next season Burnside called in Houdini and they did that stinky vanish of an elephant. The publicity was so good that even Joe Dunninger would have been satisfied with it. But how disappointing and sickening a trick. People become disgusted when their time is taken up with such foolish stuff, and particularly if they had paid money to get in and expect to see something.

A box as big as a garage was setting sideways, the bull elephant was escorted in by Mr. Houdini and the door was closed. The box was then squared around on the stage by about 30 men pulling on a block and tackle (showmanship...I wonder). The audience now had an end view of the box, the door closed. The circular openings in the front and back doors were uncovered giving a clear view through the box. These openings were not very large compared with the ends, and anyone could easily imagine the bull laying on the floor, with his back against the side wall, and they were seeing right over him. ...And why not?

It was so lousy that I was never curious about it, but it was probably a mirror, as in the diagram. Take a little mirror, set it on the drawing and you

see it works. Quite an ingenious idea if there was
any trick to be made with it.

Jarrett didn't actually propose that the elephant
had been laying on the floor of the box. Instead, he included a sketch of a mirror, improbably placed at a
shallow angle inside of the long box. In fact, readers
who attempted to place a mirror on the drawing would
easily see how it didn't work; the reflections inside the
box went wildly out of place, unlike the neat way that
45-degree angle mirrors operated in magic illusions.

It was uncharacteristic of Jarrett to be so wrong
about a principle or so speculative about something involving his livelihood. He never claimed to have seen
the illusion; in fact, he was living in California during
Houdini's appearance. Was Jarrett's description written
on good authority, or was he dismissive simply because
he didn't know?

Houdini presented the illusion during the early
months of 1918 as an addition to the Hippodrome's
review, *Cheer Up*, and his own description of the illusion was contributed to *The Sphinx* magazine.

I use a cabinet about eight feet square, about
twenty-six inches off the floor; it is rolled on by
twelve men. I show all parts, opening back and
front. The elephant walks into it; I close the doors
and curtains—doors in the back and curtains in
the front—and in two seconds I open the back and
front and she is gone. No special background, in
full glare of the lights, and it is a weird trick. In

> *fact, everyone says, "We don't see enough of it."*
> *They are so busy watching for false moves that*
> *though the trick takes seven or eight minutes, it*
> *appears like a few seconds. ...Everything is in*
> *bright light; it is no "black art" and it is a won-*
> *derful mystery for an elephant to be manipulated,*
> *they move so slowly.*

Houdini's account should be suspected of hy-perbole, but his exaggerations can be found in expected places. A key is that the cabinet was "about twenty-six inches off the floor," quite precise, but "about eight feet square," nicely vague and short of one dimension to describe a cabinet. The "two second" duration was also an improbable boast. As the entire illusion occupied seven or eight minutes, Houdini omitted the detail of the cabinet being turned or moved during its presenta-tion.

Clarence Hubbard, who gave the illusion an en-thusiastic review in *The Sphinx*, admitted that "the Hippodrome, being of such a colossal size, only those sitting directly in front got the real benefit of the de-ception. The few hundred people sitting around me took Houdini's word for it that the 'animile' had gone. We couldn't see into the cabinet at all!"

Obviously, the illusion was not well suited to that stage, and—better in descriptions than in person—was most effective at generating publicity. The Van-ishing Elephant remained, according to illusionist Servais LeRoy, a man whose comments were careful and seldom unkind, "perfect in [its] utter weakness."

Many magicians believed that the secret involved the elephant remaining in the cabinet. The standard joke at the time was that three men pushed the cabinet onto stage, the elephant entered and disappeared, then twenty men pushed the cabinet off-stage. But beyond that, no one knew positively how Houdini accomplished this illusion. The combination of Houdini, an elephant, the New York Hippodrome (he presented it for nineteen weeks and it must have been seen by nearly a million people) have combined to make this an annoying—almost preposterous—problem for historians.

I tried to solve the problem from another angle. Houdini had purchased a number of illusions from Charles Morritt around 1913 or 1914. At the time Houdini had planned to stage his own magic show; the Morritt illusions formed important parts of his repertoire. A number of magicians and writers believed that Houdini's Vanishing Elephant was actually a Morritt creation. For example, in a 1933 letter to Charles Carter, Cyril Yettmah, the English illusion inventor, wrote that "Powers [the trainer of the Race-Powers Elephants] supplied the Elephant for that very *weak* illusion, Vanishing Elephant of the late Harry Houdini's. This was only a poor elaboration of Charlie Morritt's Vanishing Donkey." Sidney Clarke, in *The Annals of Conjuring,* wrote that "in 1918 [Morritt] announced the presentation of a new mystery, 'The Disappearing Elephant,' which was exhibited in America by the late Harry Houdini."

I naturally assumed that it would be possible to find a solution to Houdini's illusion through Morritt.

After all, very few modern stage illusions remained secrets. Every illusion was tied to existing principles. Partly this was because a change of presentation could effectively change the audience's perception of a trick. The effects themselves changed quickly, but principles, concealed within the effects, could afford to evolve more slowly. A knowledgeable magician could recognize the fingerprints of a secret within an effect. The "X" or diagonal line pattern on a prop is one of those fingerprints; magicians instinctively feel the presence of a 45-degree mirror. Somewhere within the Donkey and Elephant illusions would be similar clues, linking to other stage illusions which evolved with the same secret. It seemed to me simple detective work to find the common traits: Charles Morritt's fingerprints.

•

Charles Morritt was born in 1860 in Yorkshire, the son of a gentleman farmer. He left school at an early age and rejecting the usual, expedient jobs which were available, found himself attracted to variety entertainments.

The impetus with Morritt, as with many of his generation, was the exciting, controversial program of the Davenport Brothers. Morritt read of their famous cabinet seance and in 1877, while he was living in Leeds, developed his own magical cabinet to cause someone to disappear. This he sold, through *The Era*, to a touring company.

The following year, 1878, he devoted his efforts towards his own show. "I had the courage, or audacity, to make my first a full two hours' entertainment at the Public Hall, Selby, Yorks, with no other person on the bill." He presented a series of effects, deeply entrenched Victorian conjuring like catching half-crowns in the air and tossing them into a hat, a rabbit production, lightning sketches, a cabinet seance and contact mindreading.

Morritt was employed in a minor position at the City Varieties Music Hall, Leeds, which provided an opportunity to associate with the conjurers who performed there. From the English Dobler he received lessons in the art. At the same time he was intrigued by the economics of the theatre business. Even at an early age he was something of an impresario, and by his twenty-first birthday owned two and managed some half-dozen music halls in the north of England.

In 1886, on the success of their innovative mindreading act, Morritt and his sister Lillian were brought to London with the Charles Duval Entertainment. For six months they played at Prince's Hall in Piccadilly, then spent an additional six months touring the Halls.

Morritt had perfected a "silent" second sight act, in which the coding of objects was actually accomplished through specific periods of silence, a daunting and meticulous process. The mindreading act brought Morritt to America, where he performed under contract to H. W. Williams at the Pittsburgh Academy of Music in 1887. There, Alexander Herrmann saw him

and gave him a contract for his season at Niblo's
Garden Theater, New York City.

In 1888 he returned triumphant, with the most
elegant tinge of a transatlantic accent. By the following
year he had joined the company of Maskelyne and
Cooke at Egyptian Hall, England's permanent magic
theatre. There, Morritt's energy and creativity were
highly appreciated. Mr. Maskelyne coined a new word
by billing him "The most accomplished Prestigator
(sic) of the present day."

Morritt provided an unusual, charismatic figure
on the stage, a favorite of audiences. He was well over
six feet tall, slender and imposing, with a mane of dark
hair brushed back from his forehead, an aquiline nose,
trim mustache and a bright, ready smile. A portrait of
this time shows an upturned head and distant expres-
sion, slightly haughty perhaps, but not unbecoming for
a great magician. Most notable was his characteristic
theatrical energy, a verve and dispatch which moved
him determinedly from effect to effect.

Reading opinions of his performances, it is clear
today that Morritt walked a fine line. Charles Waller
wrote, "His style was most fascinating, for he performed in a spirited, dashing fashion, as though under
the influence of strong but pleasurable excitement." But
Waller also noted the sacrifice. "At this period, he un-
doubtedly worked too fast. He drew little applause,
since he dashed rapidly from one feat to another, with
no consideration of the cheaper tricks of showmanship."

Later in his career, this tendency expanded with
Morritt's focus on new ideas and self-promotion. The

performances themselves could be quite perfunctory, infused with a cheap energy to overcompensate. S. H. Sharpe, who saw a Morritt performance in 1918, complained about the conclusion of his thought-reading act, in which the medium merely recited a pre-arranged list of articles. "Unfortunately, he moved along the front row of stalls so rapidly, while the lady rattled off the list of names...that the result was completely unconvincing. I got the impression that Morritt pointed to anything at random...." Wodehouse Pittman, reporting on Morritt's shows from the same era, was similarly aghast. "Too much noise...too much pistol shooting," he wrote.

Morritt's years with Maskelyne were invaluable, and he expanded the range of his magic. An important influence was undoubtably Buatier DeKolta, the French magician and inventor who was a favorite at Egyptian Hall during these years. Morritt and DeKolta became friends and even shared a rooming house in London. Speaking to the Magician's Club of London years later, Morritt asked if the members realized who was primarily responsible for the growth in magic's esteem. "Buatier DeKolta was the man," he continued. "A great inventor and a great performer...one of the most modest of men...he it was who first used the word 'illusionist' on a program, and who first produced illusions on the great modern scale. ...At once salaries began to rise."

A typical Morritt program before the turn of the century was a wonderful mix of conjuring, and the DeKolta influence was apparent. He would open with a signature effect, stepping on stage with a wooden embroidery hoop, about eighteen inches in diameter, stretched with tissue paper. He spun the hoop between his hands, then supported it between his left hand and shoulder. With his empty right hand he quickly reached through the paper, producing a large bouquet of tissue flowers.

Morritt proceeded with billiard ball multiplication, handkerchief productions, and the Soup Plates and Handkerchiefs (all DeKolta effects with Morritt touches). He also performed card sleights, finishing with his own version of the floating table, a large board which defied gravity and clung to his fingertips. He included hypnotic effects, like the Electric Chair routine, in which members of the audience found it difficult to sit in a chair because of a suggested electrical spark. Morritt presented hand shadows and, at Egyptian Hall, his sister Lillian took part in the Maskelyne magic plays.

On September 29, 1891 a new illusion was premiered at Egyptian Hall; it was entitled Oh!, or the Mahatmas Outdone, and was the joint invention of Morritt and Nevil Maskelyne. (Their 1891 patent indicates that the basic invention may have been planned as a pseudo-spiritual effect.) Oh!, an appropriate title for the expletive-inducing illusion, was the next generation of DeKolta's Vanishing Lady. The Maskelyne touch may have been the challenging presentation. A committee of men from the audience were invited on stage. An assistant was secured in an odd wooden chair raised on two pedestals; one arm was strapped down, one hand secured to a rope overhead, his feet raised on a shelf. The committee took the necessary steps to insure that the man did not escape. Yet, when a curtain was lowered around the man, he disappeared in a fraction of a second. The surrounding committee was left dumbfounded.

Morritt's work at Maskelyne's may have ended duet to a certain restlessness, present throughout his career. After three years Morritt left Egyptian Hall to assemble a competitive show at nearby Prince's Hall.

The Prince's Hall show, like many of his adventures in self-management, was only a moderate success. The show, in the early part of 1894, was notable for his featured co-star, the Tichborne Claimant. He was a troublesome litigant who, through the 1860s and 70s, had been in the public eye by claiming to be the heir to the Tichborne family fortune. Failed in his court case, the Claimant was drawn to increasingly desperate ways of earning a living. At Prince's Hall, he was strapped into a chair, hoisted in the air, and quickly disappeared as the stage lights were dimmed and instantly restored. This was Morritt's presentation of the Robinson illusion, Out of Sight. The London public must have been delighted by the spectacle. After the Claimant fulfilled his contract, Morritt ingeniously secured another minor celebrity—a Mr. Ted Scott, who should have figured prominently in a notorious trial the previous December but had managed to disappear from the court. Morritt's new Missing Man substituted Scott for the Claimant and kept the magician in the headlines.

Morritt's next three successes—three amazing illusions in quick sucession—earned him long engagements at the Empire Theatre, Leicester Square. The first of these was Flyto, Morritt's transposition effect using two large wooden cages. The second effect, in invented in 1893, was entitled The Convict's Escape. This utilized a piece of apparatus called The Morritt Cage, two nested cages of open bars. Notably, it was Morritt's first real success using mirrors to accomplish an effect, and the result provided further inspiration. The Flying Lady was next, a sideshow levitation illusion which he chanced to see at the Crystal Palace. Morritt quickly purchased the apparatus and presented it on the Music Hall stage.

Both Flyto and The Cage illusion were highly imitated in their day. (Flyto may have been uniquely unoriginal for Morritt; it seems to have been only a slight variation on Chevalier Thorn's suspended cabinet illusion.) Kellar and Devant, for example, presented versions of The Cage in their own shows. In fact, it was Morritt's original Cage, as seen in The Convict's Escape, which inspired a young P.T. Selbit. Selbit had picked a lock to make surreptitious visits to the basement shop where Morritt was rehearsing the illusion. There he studied its construction. Watching its performance at the London Pavilion, Selbit felt "a parental interest steal guiltily over us."

By 1895 Morritt had also achieved renown as a "hypnotist." One successful stunt guaranteed controversy and interested spectators. At the Royal Aquarium and Crystal Palace he presented A Man in a

Trance, a spectator supposedly hypnotized to remain motionless for days or weeks at a time. The London performance created debate among prominent physicians and politicians, and Home Secretary (later Prime Minister) Asquith "kindly consented to a continuation of Mr. Morritt's Experiments," according to a later playbill. A showman like Morritt could not have asked for a more distinguished endorsement.

It was an old friend, the former comic and impresario Harry Rickards, who took Morritt to Australia for eight months in 1897 as part of a vaudeville company. Years before, Rickards had been engaged by Morritt at the Leeds music hall. During the Australian tour, Morritt presented conjuring and two illusions, The Convict's Escape, and Turkish Delight. The latter was an improvement over the original Cage illusion, using a framework hung with coarse, transparent netting. Four paper frames were slid into uprights and, in quick succession, four Turkish ladies burst through the paper, magically produced.

Morritt's developments continued after his return. One effect, which earned him some renown in magic history, was presented at the London Pavilion in 1902. Four assistants supported a large board between them, waist high. There was no table involved, just the square, flat plank held by the men. A small girl stood atop the board. According to the account in Mahatma, "a screen is held in front for a second, then flung violently to the ground, folded flat, and the girl has vanished."

Morritt toured continuously in the early years of the century, moving from one small town to another. From 1903 to 1905 he sometimes worked with a blind memory man who was able to answer questions and supply obscure facts in response to the audience.

For five or six years, the dreariest of his career, Morritt effectively disappeared, working in provincial museums or halls. London magicians lost track of him and, when touring, didn't cross his path. Certainly, most thought that he was dead, probably because he had been known for bouts of drinking which had severely jeopardized his work and his health. There is reason to believe that, in the years from 1906 to 1912, Morritt was battling on many fronts: improvising promotions to pay his expenses, attempting to conquer his alcoholism, and experimenting with new principles. By now, Morritt couldn't have looked on these principles as mere curiosities, but as the lifelines which would pull another audience in place.

In 1911 he topped the bill at the Pickard's British Museum, Waxwork and Zoo in Trongate, Glasgow, promoting A Man in a Trance. Further on the same bill is a trained animal act, a chimpanzee duo named Solomon and His Wife. The name might have stuck with Morritt.

David Devant is owed the credit for rediscovering him. Devant was touring in 1912, appearing at the Hippodrome in Newcastle, and chanced to motor over to the village of Hexham to visit an old employee. During their conversation, Devant learned that there was a conjurer in town by the name of Morritt.

"This rather surprised me, because we all thought Charles Morritt was dead. No one had heard of him for years," Devant later wrote. He was taken around to the empty shop where the show was being given. The sign had Morritt's name beneath the title, The Disappearing Donkey. Devant quickly found himself face to face with Morritt, stepped inside and asked to see the donkey disappear. He did, then engaged his old acquaintance for St. George's Hall. It was as if Solomon the donkey would carry Morritt back to London, triumphant again.

Devant may have felt he was returning a favor to Morritt: years before Devant had been denied an audition with Maskelyne because of Morritt's continuing success at Egyptian Hall. When Morritt left that theatre, Devant found the opportunity which secured his career. He also must have found a kindred spirit in the magician. Both Morritt and Devant were rare combinations of conjurer, manipulator, inventor and producer which could have only been produced by the halcyon days of the last century.

Solomon first appeared on the Maskelyne stage in 1912. Later the illusion was taken on tour by Devant, who accompanied a donkey named Magic. A perfect reconstruction of the illusion is nearly impossible, as the few accounts which we have are contradictory. One reason may be that the illusion itself, like other Morritt inventions, evolved with each version. Devant's donkey stable was much more complicated, with a series of doors, upper and lower, across the back. From Elcock illustrations of the cabinets and accounts of the presentation, Devant's cabinet also had a peaked roof and was larger, proportionally, than the original. Morritt suspended a hoop at the back of the cabinet; it may have been Devant who introduced the second hoop, beneath it. (When Morritt himself exhibited the effect after his association with St. George's Hall, he used an assistant holding a "white sheet arrangement" at the back of the stage. Presumably this barrier took the place of the suspended hoop.)

The illusion held an understandable fascination for audiences. By 1912, the agrarian sensibilities had not escaped city residents; the qualities of a donkey were still apparent to everyone. Here was a notoriously intractable animal that could somehow disappear in a moment. "Mr. Morritt says he has to depend on the donkey working the mechanism for the trick," _The Magic Wand_ reported in its review. That certainly seemed to be the case, as the donkey was dramatically left inside the cabinet by itself.

In later years the Donkey was presented by a series of Maskelyne performers, including John Warren and Edward Victor. The nature of the beast invited various misadventures. Once it escaped backstage, just before its turn, and was rediscovered by a group of assistants and policemen, headed by Jasper Maskelyne, wandering the streets of London. Once in Yorkshire, as the provincial company played the Doncaster Palace, the donkey made a similar escape, heading for the railway station. On another occasion, the animal made it safely to the stage, but the mechanism had not been set properly (the technician was dozing). Edward Victor marched the donkey into the cabinet, recognized the problem, and turned to address the audience. "I promised to show you a disappearing donkey, so I had better walk off the stage myself!" He did.

•

A series of Morritt illusions, or Morritt and Devant collaborations, followed. These creations clearly represented the opportunities Morritt found at St. George's Hall, and suggested a discovery being played out in different forms. Beauty and the Beast was a production of two people atop a large, octagonal table. Ragtime Magic, which was presented in 1913, used a wide table, extending right to left across the stage, to produce four people from as many framework boxes. Devant performed the premiere of this illusion, and during the applause introduced Morritt as the inventor.

The Pillar Box Mystery, or From Pillar to Post (Nevil Maskelyne's title for the scene) was the next Morritt illusion, the subject of a 1913 patent by Morritt and Devant. Two round post boxes accomodated a series of transpositions using a cast of three.

In The Great Safe Mystery, (exhibited by Archie Maskelyne as Telepathy, False and True) objects collected from the audience were placed in a box and locked inside a Chubb safe, which remained isolated on stage. The medium easily identified the objects. Black and White consisted of a small wooden cupboard, barely large enough to contain a person, which could slide forward and backwards on a raised table. In quick succession, two assistants were produced from within it. The Panel was the production of a ghost (an assistant in gauzy costume) from a thin, upright panel of wood.

As prolific as he had been for Maskelyne and Devant, Morritt found a new champion in Harry Houdini. Will Goldston claimed that he was responsible for the partnership. Houdini was interested in assembling a magic show and was looking for "an illusion inventor who can keep a secret." Goldston recommended Morritt.

Houdini was a frustrated magician. A success in his own field of escapes, he wished to present a more traditional magic show and be accepted as a first-rate conjurer. In fact, Houdini was not well suited to the role of magician; his trademark challenging personality left little room for the necessary finesse. The artistic Servais LeRoy wrote of his friend:

> *He had a pleasing stage presence but was in no sense a finished magician, although this detail never seemed to trouble him. ...As an illusionist he never left the common place, his illusions were anything but subtle [and I] was finally forced to the conclusion that his want of originality was the answer. Using other men's ideas he was unable to improve on the original and was forced to let it go at that or produce something still weaker.*

In 1913 and 1914, Houdini assembled his show with effects from Hermalin, Goldston (the DeKolta Expanding Die), and DeVere (the Robert-Houdin

Crystal Cash Box). From Morritt came several fascinating illusions.

Goodbye Winter, the first Morritt effect, consisted of a stack of tables of decreasing size, a sort of pyramid which had been assembled on the stage. A young lady climbed a ladder, slipped underneath a cloth which covered the topmost table, then disappeared as the cloth was pulled away. "Vanishing a living, breathing human being in mid-air in the center of the stage, away from all the curtains, and in full glare of the light, in less than one-millionth of a second," Houdini's billing proclaimed.

Hello Summer, consisted of a cabinet about six feet tall, trapezoidal in shape (like an obelisk with the top cut off). Morritt later described it as a truncated pyramid. This was standing on a table so that the audience could see beneath it. Houdini tipped the cabinet forward, so the top, small end faced the audience. Because the top and bottom were open (the bottom had a grill of vertical slats), the audience could see through it to the backdrop. He righted the cabinet and, using a line from above, quickly pulled a lady from within the apparatus.

As part of his 1914 show, Houdini presented another Morritt illusion, Lady Godiva, which posters described as "amazingly vanishing a pony and rider." Houdini also purchased the Disappearing Donkey from Morritt, and a copy of Black and White, but presumably never used these two effects. From a Morritt letter it is clear that the Donkey and Pony illusions were distinct effects.

Houdini's Grand Magical Revue was not a success. The revue played only assorted dates in the spring and summer of 1914. These were obvious try-outs at Provincial theaters, a sort of "split week," featuring the Water Torture Cell on Monday through Wednesdays and the *Magic Revue* on Thursdays through Saturdays. Houdini reluctantly returned to his specialty. "If the English want escapes, they can have them," he told his friend Will Goldston. "But I am determined to give a good magic show before I die."

The equipment was shipped back to America and in 1917 Houdini again schemed to present a magic show. These plans seem to have resolved themselves in his January 1918 appearance at the Hippodrome, where he presented The Vanishing Elephant.

In 1922, while promoting his film *The Man from Beyond*, Houdini presented a brief magical revue at the Times Square Theater in New York. Included was Goodbye Winter, and Hello Summer. As a special feature, he revived his popular Vanishing Elephant. Houdini introduced the feat by calling for all the scenery to be removed. In the glare of the lights, backed with only the plain brick wall of the theater, the effect became a challenge. Houdini marched an elephant named Fannie Ringling on stage (she was a slightly smaller beast than the Hippodrome's Jennie), and escorted her into the magic cabinet. In a moment the front and back of the cabinet were opened, and the audience gazed through the box to the brick wall.

Houdini returned to magic in 1926 during his last tour, a program offering equal parts of conjuring, escapes and Spiritualism exposures. There the two Morritt effects, Summertime and Wintertime (their newly shortened titles) were included.

•

After three years of working in London and the Provinces under Maskelyne and Devant, Morritt left the partners to return to his own enterprises. His drinking, "John Barleycorn," as they called the problem politely, was still a concern among his associates, and could have affected his business decisions. The split must have represented some difficulty for David Devant, who had brought the inventor and performer to St. George's Hall, only to have Morritt leave and work in opposition.

Morritt introduced a new illusion, Tally Ho! in New Brighton in 1915. In September of that year, when a theatre at the London Polytechnic became available, he opened in competition to Maskelyne and Devant, presenting matinee shows.

This was originally in partnership with the American illusionist Carl Hertz, and the *Morritt and Hertz Mysteries*, "The Greatest Combination of Mystifiers the World has ever seen" opened on September 27, 1915. In many ways it was a repeat of his previous scheme at Prince's Hall. Again, his posters went up within view of the Maskelyne Theater as the Polytechnic was virtually across the road on Regent Street. The effort was short lived. After several weeks the partners left and although the performances continued as *Morritt's Mysteries*, a number of different magicians presented turns. (Neither this venture nor the name Morritt appeared in Hertz's colorful autobiography.) Within two months Morritt was forced to close the show.

Morritt's part of the program varied slightly during his run, but generally included an abbreviated Pillar Box Mystery, duck productions, flower productions from a trapezoidal box (quite clearly a small version of Morritt's Hello Summer for Houdini), The Disappearing Donkey, mental effects, Black and White, Laying The Ghost (Devant's ghost vanish while surrounded by a committee of spectators), hypnotic stunts, card and coin sleights. This last was a favorite effect, Morritt's Purse Trick, based on the old racecourse swindle. Working to two gentlemen from the audience, the magician transposed two copper coins, locked in a small purse, with a silver coin. The manipulation involved (the Purse Palm or Morritt Palm, it has come to be called) was unusual and delicate; the notion of performing a coin trick on stage was one of pure bravado.

Morritt's finale was his latest feature, Tally Ho! In effect, a large "4 poster arrangement" (of collapsible metal gates and yellow silk curtains) was brought on stage and shown empty. The curtains were drawn and, after a few moments, opened again to show the members of an entire foxhunt. Wodehouse Pitman, who saw the premiere of the effect in London, recorded a girl in velvet on the back of the horse, two huntsmen and a hound.

When he left the show at the Polytechnic in October of 1915, Morritt appeared for a week at the Penge Empire in suburban London. In addition to selections from his traditional repertoire, "The Great Morritt," as he was then billed, presented a playlet entitled *Forty Winks*. This was an elaboration on Tally Ho!, a scene in which Tod Sloan, a popular former jockey, was produced on horseback.

Into the twenties, Morritt's health declined. Ironically The Man in a Trance, a money-maker in meagre times, became his downfall. In October 1927 he exhibited in Halifax at the Victoria Hall, sharing the bill with the film of the week. But the local authorities discovered the deception behind The Man in a Trance. A local resident had been recruited to volunteer for the stunt, and was instructed on how to pretend to be hypnotized, how to lie motionless in a coffin, how to be awakened on stage. (Between performances he resided in a room of the theatre, where he took his meals.) At the end of the week, Morritt would solicit donations from the audience, in support of the family man who had supposedly volunteered for the trance. These donations were then split between the magician and his accomplice.

An inspector followed Morritt and his niece to Pudsey, where, on October 28, he saw the latest Man in a Trance. The policeman examined the man in the coffin, tickling his feet and lifting his eyelid to touch the eyeball. This made the man open his eyes. Morritt and his associates were arrested and charged with obtaining money under false pretenses. On November 8, 1927, the 68-year old showman first appeared in court. The evidence was unclear. Perhaps the man was in a bit of a trance when out of the coffin; perhaps the donation of money (slightly less than twenty pounds) was necessary for expenses and genuinely offered by the audience. When the the case went to trial, on January 20, 1928, it was dismissed within an hour. "The public voted it was a good show for the money, anyhow," reported *The Magic Wand*. But the victory was, by that time, a mere technicality. Morritt had been hospitalized in the months before the trial and had depleted his money between these medical and legal emergencies. He retired to Morecambe with his niece, a fortune teller, where he worked on ideas for illusions. Morritt's health never returned. In 1936, long forgotten by the London magicians, he died at Chorley on April 10, a victim of pulmonary tuberculosis. There were suggestions that he had written, then lost, an autobiography. A bit of it may have been given to Devant for inclusion in his book, *Secrets of My Magic*. But Morritt certainly never explained the extent of his mysteries or the range of his discoveries.

•

Writing after his death, Morritt's friend Frederic Culpitt listed Morritt's three fascinations: personal management, titles, and mirrors. Clearly his abilities at self-management and promotion were capable, if sometimes disappointing and expedient. His attention to titles, which undeniably drew the public, showed a particular understanding of his craft. But when Morritt turned his attention to mirrors, the results were nothing short of alchemy. His wife Adelaide reported that Morritt used to retire for the evening with pieces of looking glass under his pillow. In bed he would arrange them and rearrange them, "in an effort to discover something fresh."

What he discovered were not works of geometry but works of insight. His secrets were kept for the better part of a century, not by protecting them or locking them away, but within a cloud of endless, breathless creativity, Morritt's honest attempts to put something new before the public. He hid his secrets, the way all magicians must, in plain sight.

Notes

I've made an effort to construct a complete, if by no means definitive, biography of Morritt. The sources tell fractional, often conflicting parts of his life. This account of the Donkey illusion has been assembled from *The Magic Wand* review from September of 1912, the Elcock sketches from the same month in *The Magician's Monthly*, John Salisse and John Davenport's *A Candid View of the Maskelynes, 1916-1917*, and a manuscript copy of Devant's patter for the effect (a performance from December 1914), which was graciously shown to me in a private collection. The most helpful sketch of the apparatus is an elaborate Elcock illustration for the front of the "To-day 1914" issue of *The Magic Mirror*, David Devant's promotional paper. I have never found an actual copy of this, but it is reproduced in the December 1944 *Sphinx*.

Jarrett's history with the Vanishing Elephant is from his book, *Jarrett Magic*, 1936, which was republished with annotations by this author in a Magic Inc. edition, *Jarrett*, 1981. The Houdini and Clarence Hubbard accounts are from the March 1918 *Sphinx* Magazine; Servais LeRoy's remarks are from *Monarch of Magic*, 1984, by William V. Rauscher. The Yettmah letter, to Charles Carter, is in Mike Caveney's collection.

Morritt's biography has been compiled from a number of sources: his own early account appears as an appendix to Devant's *Secrets of My Magic*, 1936. Other articles and drawings appear in Waller and Taylor's *Magical Nights at the Theatre*, 1980, and *The Magician Monthly* for September 1913, November 1913, February 1914 and March 1914, and *The Wizard* for September 1905. A photo of his donkey and clown appeared in the February 1913 *The Magician Monthly*. A short biography appeared in Goldston's *Who's Who in Magic*. Early Morritt programs appeared in Burrows' *Programmes of Magicians* and Stanyon's *Magic* for August 1902, and there are many brief mentions of his appearances through the volumes of *Mahatma*.

By far the most useful series of Morritt articles were Charles Waller's "Memories of Morritt" in March-May 1940 *Magic Wand*, followed by Frederic Culpitt's "Regarding Charles Morritt" in the October-November 1940 issue of the same magazine, and a letter in the June-September 1941 issue. Jack Ledair wrote on Morritt in the April 5, 1952 *Abracadabra*.

Other Morritt stories appear in Devant's *My Magic Life*, 1931, and Rae Hammond's *The Magic of Edward Victor's Hands*, 1995. The 1911 Morritt appearance is from a bill in my collection. The early Morritt portrait appeared in *The Encore*, November 24, 1893.

Hercat in his book, *Latest Conjuring*, 1913, described a silent second sight act which an unnamed magician attempted to sell him. From the circumstances, he was describing Morritt. Hercat later discerned the secret. S.H. Sharpe's recollections are from his book *Conjurer's Psychological Secrets*, 1988.

The Graphic for March 10 and April 14, 1894 describe the Vanishing Claimant and The Missing Man—Morritt's celebrity illusions.

It is interesting to speculate whether Morritt's invention with the board and four men was the inspiration for an intriguing but mythical illusion: the disappearance of a lady on a sheet of glass. (Supposedly the lady climbs into one of the men, a hollow dummy supporting the glass.) This was described in Gibson and Young's *Houdini on Magic*, 1953.

The Houdini connection is explained in Goldston's *Secrets of Famous Illusionists*. The Houdini illusions are described in Clinton Burgess' review in the May 1922 *Sphinx*. A bill advertising Lady Godiva appeared in Milbourne Christopher's *Houdini, A Pictorial Life*, 1976, as did an unsourced bill reproduced by The Houdini Historical Center in Appleton, Wisconsin. A Morritt letter to Houdini mentioned the donkey and pony illusions, explaining how the donkey illusion should end with the performer raising the roof to show it empty. Hardeen offered the Disappearing Donkey for sale in *The Conjurer's Magazine*, Volume 1, number 1. According to the ad, it was built "by Charles Morret (sic) in England."

Houdini wrote of Morritt in a series of letters to Kellar; I was able to view these in the collection of David Copperfield. Although it was widely understood that The Vanishing Elephant was a Morritt idea, to the best of my knowledge the master publicist Houdini never mentioned the origins of this illusion, even to his friend Kellar.

I was lucky enough to know Vic Torsberg and Orson Welles; both had both seen Houdini's magic act as part of his final tour. "It was a stage full of push button

German crap," Torsberg told me. "Bad stuff." Welles, eleven years old at the time, was taken to the same tour by his father. He thrilled to the escapes and spiritualism exposures, but was horrified by the magic. "Houdini walked out on the stage and started by pulling off his sleeves...ripping off the sleeves of his tailcoat! 'No sleeves,' you know, that sort of thing," he once told me, making a suitable face as he recalled the show. "Can you imagine, a short sleeve tail coat and his bare arms? Even as a kid I realized the coarseness of it. Then he proceeded to perform a bunch of mechanical effects...by no stretch of the imagination were his sleeves involved."

Accounts of the Polytechnic show appear in *The Magic Wand* for October 1915 and in Davenport and Salisse's, *A Candid View of the Maskelynes, 1916-1917*, 1995. In this book, Wodehouse Pittman's letters to Devant express a very poor opinion of Morritt. From his descriptions, the Polytechnic show does seem a disappointing affair, though Pittman's sarcastic tone with Morritt suggests that he was playing to his audience: Devant. Perhaps there was understandable bitterness about Morritt leaving and setting up a rival show, especially if Devant felt he had reintroduced Morritt to success in London.

The account of Morritt's arrest in Halifax is from the local papers. David Britland kindly accepted the mission to explore library files for the story. A Selbit form letter, an appeal for funds on Morritt's behalf, is in the David Copperfield collection. There are also brief mentions of the incident in the 1928 issues of *The Magic Wand*.

5. Mister Morritt's Donkey (In Practice)

One measures a circle, beginning anywhere.
—*Charles Fort*

Alan Wakeling retired in 1987. After his own career performing in nightclubs and theaters, he had been the creative director with Mark Wilson Productions, responsible for designing Mark's new illusions and supervising his shows. Magicians appreciated his clear, graceful innovations and his ability to assess a problem and solve it theatrically. Although he had stopped per-

forming years before, he never lost the sense of the performance—like a choreographer who used to be a
featured dancer and knew how every step would be received.

The month after his retirement, I visited Alan at
his home in Westlake Village and took him a surprise.
"If you really plan on having spare time..." I started.
Alan nodded. I presented him with a thick file on
Morritt. Elcock's sketches. Articles. Reviews. Interviews.
Photos of the donkey. Somewhere in this file, I reasoned, were clues to the mystery, but after years I
needed help. "I'm going to loan you this and when you
get a chance, read it over and tell me where the donkey
went. I'm not going to tell you what I think. You can
put it together yourself."

Alan kept the file for months. So long, I reasoned, that he had forgotten about the assignment or
moved on to more important things, like the small
wooden props which emerged from his workshop. One
day I was surprised to find the file in the middle of his
table.

"What do you think?" I asked.

"Well, it's an interesting problem," he said, a
casual gesture of defeat as he slid the file across the
table. Not the gesture I had hoped for. "There were
two clowns."

I didn't get it. "Why do you say that?"

"Because you wouldn't dress the assistant as a
clown unless you were doubling him with someone
else."

Alan spoke from experience. In one of his acts, a

circus illusion act, he had used clown make-up and costuming so that he could match two people.

"Okay..." I continued, feeling that Alan was getting to a punch line. "And what does that have to do with the illusion?"

"No idea," Alan said quietly. He straightened his glasses, closed the file and handed it to me.

"But wait a second, there has to be some reason...."

"Oh, I'm sure there was an important reason. But I don't know what it was. I have no idea where the donkey went. I just know that there were two clowns, because that's the only reason you'd use clown make-up in that part."

I had been looking for evidence of Morritt's famous mirrors. "Was the second clown involved in a reflection?" I asked.

"Well, that doesn't make much sense," Alan continued. "Probably no mirrors in the cabinet because the clown jumps inside. I don't see how that sort of reflection could have worked. I don't know why he needed a second clown. I don't know how the trick worked. But the secret involved two clowns."

I left that lunch with the file under my arm. I had been attempting to reconstruct the secret, trying to measure Morritt's techniques. Alan's suggestion made a mess of it all because it didn't deal with a logical formula. It was a reminder that part of the secret was the finesse of a presentation, the feints and fakes which could not be calculated, which only surrounded the geometry like a fog.

•

At the start of Morritt's career, mirror illusions were not yet thirty years old. And although the notion of an illusion "done with mirrors" has since become deadened with familiarity, it is easy to imagine how that generation was seduced with the idea and fascinated with the geometry. Pepper and Tobin had started the movement with the 1865 Sphinx illusion, the talking head on a table. The Sphinx arrangement consisted of two upright mirrors positioned at a 90-degree angle, since called "v-mirrors" because they formed the shape of that letter. The mirrors seemed to visually "grab" a section of scenery in its reflection, placing it behind the table. In this way the Sphinx's body, which was behind the mirrors, seemed invisible.

It was an effective deception. The mirrors not only blocked the body, but actually created an open space through reflection; the nature of a mirror is that we don't look at it, but look through it to something else. (A dirty or smudged mirror, by contrast, gives us something to look at in the plane of the mirror.) As long as the 45- and 90-degree angles within the set had been carefully arranged, as long as the audience could see the mirrors, they could see the reflection and appreciate the illusion.

The Protean Cabinet followed, using hinged "v-mirrors" inside a large wooden wardrobe, reflecting the

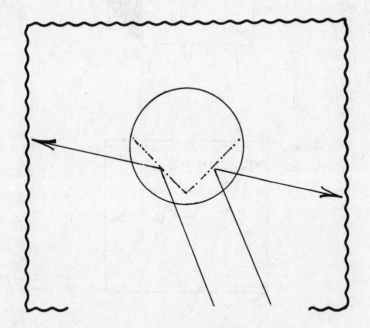

Top: The Sphinx Illusion
(The mirrors are between the table legs.)
Bottom: An overhead view of the Sphinx Illusion, showing the
sightlines which reflect off the mirrors and to the surrounding scenery.

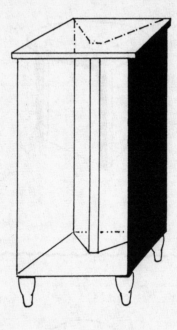

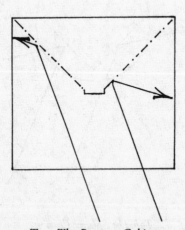

Top: *The Protean Cabinet*
Bottom: *An overhead view of the Cabinet, showing the sightlines
which reflect off the mirrors and to the interior walls.*

interior walls. Assistants standing behind the mirrors seemed to disappear. Such a cabinet involved a practical improvement. In the Sphinx effect the mirrors reflected the surrounding drapery, so it required a carefully arranged setting around it. The Protean Cabinet mirrors only reflected the foreground—the walls of the cabinet. The reflections could be arranged within the prop itself. Maskelyne's *Will, the Witch and the Watchman* cabinet used a similar arrangement within a large wooden cabinet.

In many ways the Cage illusion, Morritt's 1893 invention, was a slavish copy of the mirrors in *Will, the Watch and the Watchman*. However, the result of The Morritt Cage was breathtakingly original and insightful. The apparatus was raised up on tall legs and consisted of two nested cages, isolated in the center of the stage. Each was approximately six feet tall. The outer cage, roughly five feet square in plan, was comprised of vertical bars on the sides and back. The front was open. Centered within this was an inner cage, just wide enough to contain a person. This cage, similarly, was formed of vertical bars.

The nested cages suggested isolation; the walls of bars made the entire illusion transparent. Still, when covered momentarily, the apparatus could produce, transpose or vanish someone standing within the center cage.

In fact, an invisible wedge was formed with two upright sheets of mirror. Behind the wedge the assistant could be concealed.

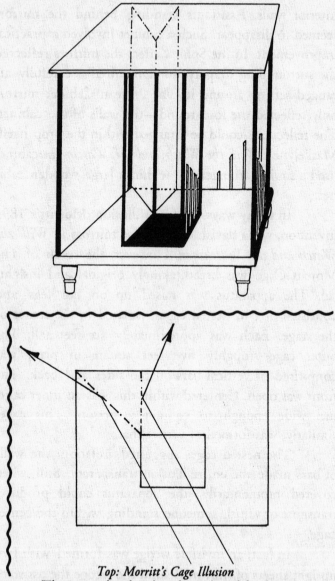

Top: Morritt's Cage Illusion
(The surrounding bars have been omitted for clarity.)
Bottom: An overhead view of the Cage Illusion, showing the sightlines
which reflect off the mirrors and to the surrounding scenery.

The diagonal sheet of glass provided most of the deception. As in the Sphinx illusion, it was mounted at a 45-degree angle to the backdrop and visually "grabbed" a section of matching drapes, at one side of the stage, to optically place them behind the cabinet. The second mirror, which was mounted perpendicular to the background, served to conceal the hidden assistant from spectators at the extreme sides and generally improve the angles at which the apparatus could be viewed. This mirror reflected a small section of the background. According to Morritt's patent drawings for the cage, this second mirror hinged open like a door, from the back edge. When the inner cage was covered with curtains or roller blinds, the assistant could secretly step inside of it.

Morritt's formula indicated an understanding of foreground and background. The original Sphinx illusion reflected only the background, the surrounding curtains. The Protean Cabinet reflected the foreground, the solid sides of the cabinet. Morritt's Cage provided a foreground object, the vertical barred walls of the cage, and a background object, the surrounding draperies seen through the cage. This guaranteed a "transparent" effect, a perfect optical illusion utilizing the mirrors.

Turkish Delight utilized a similar arrangement. Instead of the outer cage, Morritt used a framework draped with open netting. Instead of the inner cage, four narrow uprights concealed the mirror edge and supported the paper frames which produced the ladies.

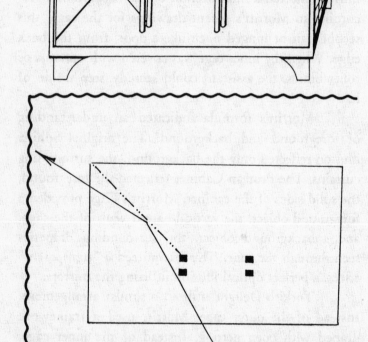

Top: Morritt's Turkish Delight
Bottom: An overhead view of the Turkish Delight cabinet, showing
the sightlines which reflect off the mirrors and to the scenery.

Charles Waller wrote that Turkish Delight used only
one mirror, the diagonal mirror, and eliminated the
perpendicular mirror. (If the apparatus were slightly
larger, the assistants could be concealed using only the
diagonal mirror.) This would have simplified the productions of each assistant, and allowed the magician to
pass behind the cabinet at one side and not cause stray
reflections.

The plank supported by four assistants,
Morritt's illusion from the London Pavilion, utilized
the same illusion principle. Beneath the square plank
was the familiar wedge of mirrors, one at 45- and one
at 90-degrees. The plank must have been roughly four
feet square. Actually, the plank was supported by the
mirrors and the framework behind them. The men
standing at the corners concealed the edges of the mirrors, and one man's left leg was reflected in place of his
right, or an entire set of legs was reflected under a different man. Morritt must have been delighted by this
artifice, as the reflections matched perfectly. As in his
Cage, an effective foreground was provided by the
men's legs. The background was the surrounding scenery.

•

Morritt's career can be analyzed as the efficient
uses of two basic principles. Starting in the 1890s, he
utilized his wedge of mirrors, 45- and 90-degrees, as
seen in the Cage and plank illusions. Starting in 1912,
when he reappeared in London, he was using a

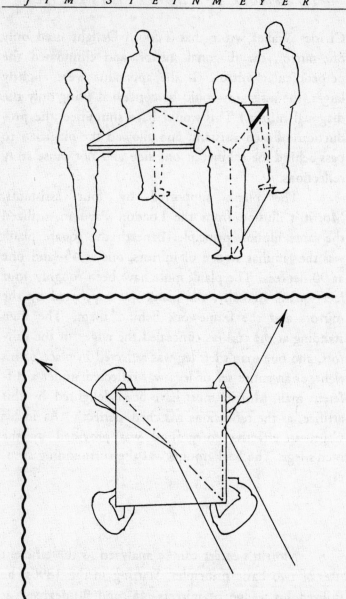

Top: Morritt's illusion with the plank supported by four assistants
Bottom: An overhead view showing the sightlines which reflect off the
mirrors and to the scenery

substantially different principle with mirrors. There's a good record of this secret, despite the fact that it has become lost or ignored by magicians.

Beauty and the Beast was developed and performed by Morritt and Devant and recorded in David Devant's *Secrets of My Magic*. As in many of his accounts, it was concisely described.

> When the curtain rose, all that was to be seen on the stage was a platform, octagonal in shape, about four feet in diameter, and looking like a huge Moorish stool. It stood about eighteen inches from the floor. On it was a large brass flower pot and behind it, leaning against the leg, was a gauze covered hoop. This, by the way, could be distinctly seen through and underneath the platform. In front of the platform was a miniature pair of steps. I commenced by stepping on to the platform using these steps and picking up the flower-pot to show the audience it was full of mold. I told them that it contained fairy seeds. I picked up the gauze covered hoop and, opening it out, it appeared to be a bell-shaped affair, which I suspended on a cord which hung above the platform. I then got off the platform and the gauze cage was lowered down to it....

According to the routine, the action shifted to a smaller effect, a miniature greenhouse which produced blooms.

I now called attention to the gauze bell which was gradually becoming transparent owning to some lights which were in the top of it, and through the gauze was seen a huge rose tree in the pot, and at the side of this was a beautiful princess in the act of plucking a rose. Behind crouched a huge beast....

Using a special costume, the beast was transformed to a prince, the gauze bell lifted and the performers stepped forward. Devant recorded the secret, a contrary bit of magical science:

I daresay you have been able to guess the secrets of this illusion. In the first place two sheets of mirror glass are placed underneath the octagonal platform. They meet at the top end, that is, the end farthest from the audience, and open out gradually towards the end nearest the audience. They are in fact open wide enough at that end for the prince to climb up through the opening provided in the stage, having climbed up on the top of the platform. (You must remember there was nothing seen through the bell until the lights were put on inside.) ....The legs not being quite enough to conceal the opening between the glasses, a small pair of steps is requisitioned, these are put in front and conceal the extra space taken up. They are put carelessly sideways so they should not be suspect.

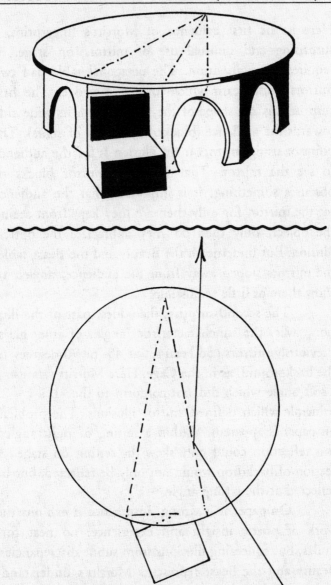

Top: Morritt's table for Beauty and the Beast
Bottom: An overhead view of the table, showing the sightlines which
reflect off the mirrors and to the scenery.

Here is the first evidence of Morritt's fingerprint, a surprising and unusual use of mirrors on stage. It requires some attention. The octagonal table had two mirrors underneath which formed a wedge. The first surprise was the shape of the wedge, with its wide side towards the audience (blocked by the set of stairs). The point of using mirrors in an illusion is for the audience to see the mirror. That is, if the mirror blocks or obscures something, it is important that the audience see the mirror, for only then are they kept from seeing the object, only then do they appreciate the optical illusion. But underneath the Beauty and the Beast table, the mirrors sloped away from the audience, angled to show them as little as possible.

The second surprise, the oddest part of the illusion, was the uncharacteristic angle of the glass. Previously mirrors had been set at 45- or 90-degrees to the background, as in the Cage. Here Morritt was using a soft angle which did not conform to the "1 + 1 = 2" principle which defined mirror illusions. The problem on paper is apparent. Within a setting of right angles, this reflection could only skew the setting on stage. A section of backdrop would not only be reflected, but be reflected at the wrong angle.

On paper it is wrong. In practice it exhibits the work of poetic insight and experience: no neat formulas, but squeezing illusions from subtle discrepancies. Beauty and the Beast represents Morritt's understanding that his equation didn't need to total two. The audience simply had to believe that it did.

Such a soft angle reaches over and "grabs" a nearby section of the backdrop; no longer did Morritt need to drape the sides of the stage for his reflections. While the mirror skews the angle of this reflection and reverses it, an audience would find it hard to notice such a discrepancy if the background was of a regular pattern. Morritt used foreground objects of particular shapes to support the reflection. Devant's clue is the reference to the gauze-covered hoop which leaned against the table leg in back. This was the prominent object the audience saw reflected in the mirrors. In fact, a flat circular shape proves the perfect answer for these slightly-skewed reflections. In Morritt's mirror, one half of the circle goes a bit oval, but the difference is almost impossible to notice. By contrast, a square shape behind the table becomes noticeably "bent."

Confirming this principle was a 1914 patent issued in Morritt's name. By now the angled mirror was used in a much more sophisticated way, showing the audience as much of it as possible and containing it within a cabinet or barrel. The patent described a trapezoidal box with an angled mirror running from one end to the other. The mirror started at the open front edge and extended to the center of the back. By looking through the enclosure, the backdrop was doubled in the reflection, giving the impression that the audience could see straight through the cabinet.

I, Charles Morritt, of 12 Bolsover Street, London W., Illusionist, do hereby declare the nature of my

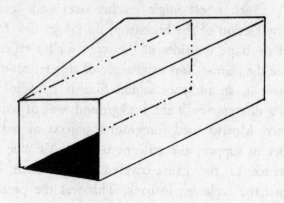

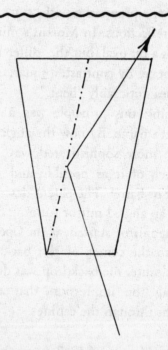

Top: *Morritt's patent for a trapezoidal box.*
Bottom: *An overhead view of the box, showing the sightlines which
reflect off the mirror and to the scenery.*

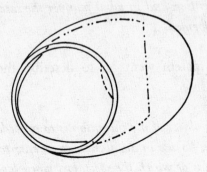

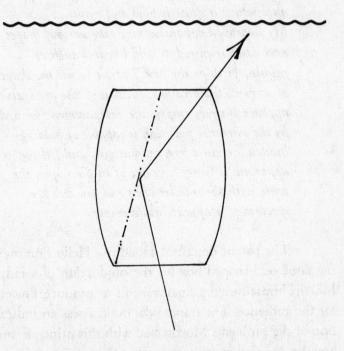

Top: Morritt's patent for a barrel with a mirror.
Bottom: An overhead view of the barrel, showing the
sightlines which reflect off the mirror and to the scenery.

invention and in what manner the same is to be performed....

His patent went on to describe the preferred cabinet.

> *The object of my invention is to provide an apparatus for use in an illusion at an entertainment by means of which the spectators when looking into the open end of...suchlike appliance shall believe that they are looking into and through an appliance which is quite hollow and empty....*
> *My improved apparatus may take various shapes and when required to hold livestock such as rabbits, birds or the like. I prefer to use the shape of a truncated pyramid... Although the apparatus appears entirely empty, the compartment formed by the mirrored partition is capable of holding hidden therein a boy, man or girl, and [if] the apparatus is lying upon one of its sides upon the table with the smaller open end towards the spectators, it appears quite empty.*

The patent described Houdini's Hello Summer, the same odd-shaped box for the production of a lady. Morritt himself used a small version to produce flowers for the audience. The trapezoidal cabinet was an indication of the problems Morritt had with this principle and how he wrestled to make it work. Once again, the mirror at this shallow angle could provide an acceptable background reflection; the backdrop, when skewed, was barely noticeable. But the foreground, the interior of the box itself, was a different problem. The mirror would have caused wild reflections inside the box. Morritt solved this with the trapezoid or pyramid-shaped container. By looking in the small end, the sides of the box angled away from the audience. They could not see the interior walls, only the area beyond the box.

A photo of Houdini on stage from his 1926 tour shows the Hello Summer apparatus pushed up against the backdrop. Behind it is a large, round paper covered hoop, suggesting that this may have been the object held behind the cabinet when it was shown empty.

The patent also described the same idea as applied to a barrel. Once again, the angled mirror started at the front edge and ran to the center of the opposite side. Such a mirror, with sides of perfectly-shaped curves, would have been especially difficult to cut and fit within the prop. But the barrel is significant because it identifies that Morritt, by the time he had filed for the patent, had found the solution to the foreground reflections: a circle. It was the perfect shape to disguise the shallow angle of the mirror. The round back edge of the barrel worked just like the circular hoop in Beauty and the Beast.

•

The long, narrow box, the angled mirror, the circular ends: the invention suggested by Morritt's patent was certainly familiar to me as Jarrett's description

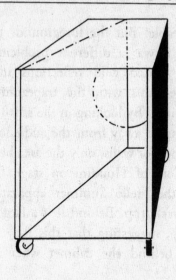

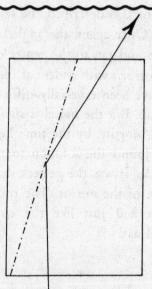

*Top: A reconstruction of Houdini's Vanishing Elephant, based on the
principle patented by Morritt.
Bottom: An overhead view of the Elephant Cabinet, showing the
sightlines which reflect off the mirror and to the scenery.*

of Houdini's Vanishing Elephant. If Jarrett proposed a possible method for the 1918 Elephant Vanish, and that method happened to match a 1914 Morritt patent, the coincidence was impossible to ignore.

I found a large plastic elephant and, working off that scale, made a plywood model based on Jarrett's description. The finished model was about 36 inches long. I fitted the mirror at Morritt's odd angle and looked inside the box. The mirror misshaped the interior walls of the cabinet. But there were obvious solutions, and wonderful results.

Morritt had earlier tried to avoid seeing the sides of the cabinet by using a trapezoidal shape. In the Elephant illusion the interior walls were simply colored flat black. The awkward reflections disappeared as the black upon black edges of the cabinet disappeared. The prominent circular opening in the back was the only focus when looking into the cabinet. This shape was the foreground in the reflection, the scenery behind it formed the background. (A narrow vertical strip, supposedly a door stop for the semicircular doors, could conceal the vertical edge of the mirror. Morritt, in his patent, described vertical slats or bars for this purpose.)

Most amazing was the way that the two semicircular doors worked with the mirror. The audience could only see one door; the second was a reflection. But the odd angle of the mirror made it appear as if the doors hinged opened at different rates. It was a powerful and convincing illusion: one door swung open just a moment after the other. I estimated that the full-sized prop would have used a mirror not larger than eight by twelve feet. This size of mirror was not only available but quite practical once mounted against a wooden wall and separated from the actual elephant.

In Houdini's effect, the large cabinet was first shown with its side to the audience. The elephant was led into one end, where she could walk directly into the wedge formed by the mirror. The two doors with half-circular cut-outs were closed behind her. The cabinet was now given a quarter turn, bringing the curtained front towards the audience. The curtains were thrown open, then the half-circular doors in back hinged open, allowing a view through the cabinet and to the scenery. This secret matched the descriptions of Houdini's illusion, including the size (8 by 8 feet at one end), the proportions and the black interior. Most telling was the prominent circular shape of the doors in the back, not only a distinctive feature of this illusion, but the mark of Morritt's principle.

My model, which I demonstrated to the Magic Collectors Association at their 1983 convention, also accounted for the failure of Houdini's Hippodrome illusion and explained why, when Jennie the elephant disappeared, so few in the audience were impressed. The illusion could only be appreciated by looking down the length of it. The interior was dark. With the back doors opened, the cabinet could not be revolved as the mirrors would cause any vertical pattern on the backdrop (like the folds of a curtain) to converge and reveal the reflection. In other words, the very nature of the illusion prevented it from being shown empty to a wide auditorium like that of the Hippodrome.

For a 1984 production of *A Christmas Carol*, I was asked by the Goodman Theater in Chicago to create the stage effects. One sequence was of childhood fantasy; the director asked if a pony could be magically produced on the stage of the Auditorium Theater. I had suspected that the Elephant illusion would make a good production, and that by closing the circular doors as the cabinet was turned, it could be nicely shown empty. I scaled up the model to pony size, approximately five feet square at the end and eight feet long, decorated like a small rustic stable. By blackening out a narrow strip near the front edge of the mirror, the angles could be adjusted so that the cabinet could be revolved without any stray reflections of the audience.

Although no patrons of the Goodman suspected it, that *Christmas Carol* production represented the solution to Houdini's famous illusion and the proof of its efficiency on a stage. For two weeks the little pony marched out of the empty cabinet to applause, and the success of the deception naturally reminded me of other Morritt puzzles. Inside that cabinet, the wedge formed by the mirror was a perfect shape for an animal like a pony, a horse or elephant. In fact, once the animal was loaded inside, there was additional room in the corners of the wedge for a little more, perhaps one or two people and a dog. Was this Tally Ho!, Morritt's production of a fox-hunt from an empty cabinet? It was tempting and logical to connect the dots. Here was a step by step evolution of the principle, each step represented as a new illusion: Morritt's patent with the trapezoidal box and barrel, Houdini's Hello Summer,

The Lady Godiva Illusion (a vanish of a pony circa 1914), Morritt's Tally Ho!, and the Vanishing Elephant.

I had inadvertently managed to solve the problem of Houdini's elephant without addressing how the Donkey disappeared. If the Donkey illusion fitted properly into this sequence, it became the "missing link" between the early Morritt illusions, like the Cage, and the later effects, like Hello Summer. I had the beginning of the equation and the end of the equation. By working both ends against the middle, there would have to be a spot where they connected.

•

Here I have two hoops covered with linen. It would be a clever donkey that could jump through this hoop without making a hole in it. (Tapping hoop taken from assistant.) One of these hoops we are going to place beneath the little stable. (Throws hoop down in front of the stable.) Put it right underneath. (Assistant hands performer hoop number 2 and places number 1 right under stable.) Those in the stalls can see that hooping the whole time and the moment the donkey has disappeared I will show it [to] you again. This other hoop I propose to hang up behind the stable on those two cords. This will prevent the Donkey jumping through the back. (Goes up stage and hooks hoop on one cord while assistant fastens the other.) Show the inside of the stable. (One assis-

tant opens the three doors in front and the other opens the upper doors at back.)

This 1914 written transcript, prepared for David Devant, was taken from his performance while on tour. It gives the best account of the Disappearing Donkey and hints at the secret. Immediately there is the fussing with the hoops, the circle shape which should be a key to the mystery. One hoop is hung behind the cabinet on ribbons and a second is slid beneath the cabinet. Does the hoop beneath the cabinet reflect in place of the hoop behind it? A 45-degree mirror would give this effect. But the idea isn't practical for many reasons. For example, the floor of the cabinet would be in the way of the reflection. More than likely, the second hoop is a feint to distract attention from the important hoop behind the cabinet. After all, there is no doubt of the donkey passing through the floor of the cabinet beneath the stage; the apparatus is clearly raised up on tall legs.

But already something significant has happened. The cabinet is not opened or shown until the hoop behind the cabinet is hung in place. In other words, the cabinet only looks right—can only be displayed—when the hoop is behind it, and the audience does not see the process of the hoop being hung. It is taken behind the cabinet (where it may show slightly above the cabinet), then the front and back are opened showing the static hoop in place.

I assure you that the donkey cannot be hurt during this experiment. (Takes hold of upper door off prompt side of stable front and also signal.) It does not hurt the donkey to be put in a stable like this. It is not like putting a donkey in a stable. Shut it up! (Assistants shut all doors and then get the run-up board. Performer shuts door he is holding and at same time gives signal. The two assistants beneath stage now raise the fake.)

The fake is the secret to the illusion: whatever its nature, it looks acceptable when it is down, but can only be raised after it is hidden from the audience's view. Also, it needs to be raised before the donkey enters the cabinet, suggesting that the donkey passes directly into or through the fake. As for the men beneath the stage, the fake must be large or cumbersome to require two men and necessitate a signal (a push button light, perhaps) from the magician. Still, there is a great deal learned from what is not written. For example, it is unlikely that the donkey exited out the back of the cabinet, as it would on a raised plank or ramp through the curtains. If there were hidden access to the cabinet from the back, wouldn't this be the most logical way to operate the secret and hide assistants? We can assume that if the assistants were concealed beneath the stage, the cabinet was positioned far from any scenery.

Also, the instructions clearly say that men raise the fake, not specifically that the fake is raised through the stage. We know only that the illusion is being operated from below. Although extravagant today, often holes would be cut in a stage to operate a mechanism. Devant's Educated Fish and A.B.C. Fly, for example, were small effects operated by cords or rods through the stage.

> *We have side doors also. (Opens the one his side.) We will put the donkey in a the side door. (By this time the run-up board has been placed in position by the assistants and they open door on the other side. Clown proceeds to lead donkey up slope and into stable going in backwards himself and in front of donkey.) And I want you to notice that all of the donkey goes in, every bit of it. (The moment the clown comes out of the stable the performer shuts the side door. The two assistants at the other side shut the other door. One assistant retires. The other stands by back doors. Performer gives signal. The assistants below lower fake.) One, two, three, and up goes the donkey! The donkey's gone! The donkey is gone! Open the doors. (During the last speeches, which are shouted, performer is listening for lowering of fake. Directly he hears it down he opens top door, off prompt side, clown runs and opens other top door and then lower ones. Assistant at back, who has been looking through, takes his cue from per-*

former opening front upper door and all three
doors at back quickly. Then, coming to side of sta-
ble quickly picks up the hoop from underneath
stable and hands it to performer.)

("Up goes the donkey" was a catchphrase of the
day, a parody of the street showmen who were always
promising a wonder.)

According to this account, the fake is opened
before the donkey enters. Soon after, the clown
emerges from the side of the cabinet, the fake is lowered by the men beneath the stage, and the cabinet can
be opened to show that the donkey is gone. Again, the
suggestion is that the fake, whatever its nature, does not
look acceptable while it is up, only when lowered.

The first impression is that the donkey itself is
being lowered through the stage, perhaps within a container or behind a piece of masking (the fake) which
passed through the floor. But I realized that taking the
donkey through the stage would be improbable.
Devant toured with the illusion. Morritt performed it
outdoors in Brighton. The equipment necessary for
such a trapdoor would have been quite beyond the ca-
pacity of any touring magic show or a seaside stage,
and more massive than any of the other Maskelyne illusions. As there was much attention to the speed of the
vanish and the sudden lack of hoofbeats, the suspicion
is that the donkey was not going far before it had disappeared.

Open the roof. The donkey's gone. (The moment
clown has opened front doors he jumps inside sta-
ble and lifts up roof. Performer takes hoop again.)

While we never saw anyone enter the cabinet
previously, at the very end the clown jumps inside;
more than likely there were no mirrors within the cabinet. Also, no performer walks behind the cabinet in
view of the audience. Only the hoop, which has not
moved during the effect, gives the effect of looking
through the apparatus.

•

From an unexpected source, one part of the illusion was suddenly solved. Alan Wakeling was right.
There were two clowns.

Jasper Maskelyne had let it slip. Writing in his
book, *White Magic*, the grandson of John Nevil
Maskelyne explained the romanticized story of his
family and anecdotes from his life as a magician.
Jasper's carelessness might be tragic if it weren't so
innocent; he had learned to tell an amusing story but
accidentally told too much.

We were presenting a trick with a donkey, but
the donkey disappeared before its time. My father
was on the stage, and I was behind the scenes
waiting to go on, when an agitated magician came
running up.

"My donkey's disappeared!" he gasped. "Some
fool's left the door open at the back, and the
damned beast has vanished. We're due to go on in
five minutes. What shall we do?"
I hastily dashed off a note to my father, said a
word to the stage manager, arranging with him to
alter the order of the program, and, assisted by
two clowns in full make-up, raced out into
Langham Place to try to trace the lost quadruped.

Jasper Maskelyne found it, "nearly half a mile
away, in Berners Street, where he was walking sedately
along."

The donkey, escorted back to the theatre by the
five constables, two clowns and myself, arrived in
time to be included as the penultimate turn of the
evening. He "did his stuff" perfectly, apparently
quite unaffected by his taste of urban excitements.

I called Alan, and we were both amazed at the
reference. In the context of the presentation, the second
clown was apparently the secret which had so intrigued
contemporary writers. The Disappearing Donkey, after
all, was fascinating because of the nature of a donkey.
Audiences expected the worst from such an animal, and
its intransigence added to the illusion. How does one
manipulate a donkey? Morritt made the most of it by
bragging about the donkey's abilities. *The Magic Wand*
reported:

Mr. Morritt says he has to depend on the donkey working the mechanism for the trick, and never once has the donkey betrayed the confidence reposed in him.

But this boast was a deception. The trainer of the donkey (probably not a performer) would be made up as a clown. Another assistant, of the same approximate size, would look identical in similar make-up. In order to give the impression that the donkey had been left alone in the cabinet—a vital bit of the presentation—the second clown rapidly left the cabinet once the donkey was pulled inside. This allowed the trainer to stay with Solomon through the entire illusion, pulling him in place or moving him through the cabinet, as necessary. All the while the audience believed that he donkey was alone, contemplating kicking apart the stable or lunging for the doors.

In fact, Solomon was no super-donkey, but required the expected attention and coercion. The audience never realized that Morritt was not merely vanishing a donkey. He was producing a clown, then vanishing a donkey with a second clown.

•

It turns out that I had been close to a solution for many years, turning and twisting the mirror principle in my notebook, sketching the possibilities. Starting from the circle hanging behind the cabinet, I interpolated a mirror at various angles, but I had not taken the principle far enough backwards. The revelation for me was that The Disappearing Donkey might be very close to the sensibility of Morritt's early Cage illusion. The mirror was not inside the cabinet but out the back, the same way that the mirrors in the Cage had been arranged on the periphery of the tiny, inner cage. Then, if the mirror were turned horizontally, so that it hinged opened like a clamshell instead of swinging open like a door—Devant's transcript said distinctly that the fake was raised—I suddenly reached a practical solution.

You can imagine a simple example of the principle, the circle as the object of the reflection. If you drink a dark beverage like coffee from a mug while gazing into the mug, there is a point at which the edge of the liquid bisects the bottom circle of the mug. The angle of the liquid then slopes down to your lips. There is a near-perfect reflection of the circular bottom of the cup; the dark liquid acts as a mirror surface. This is the reflection expressed in Morritt's patent using a barrel. This is the basis of the Disappearing Donkey.

In fact, Morritt's inspiration may have been diagrammed in an 1875 book on stagecraft. M.J. Moynet's *L'Envers du Théâtre (The Theatre Inside-Out)*, explained a number of elaborate stage effects, including changing scenery, trap doors and mirror illusions. It is one of very few books published on the subject. Moynet cited a recent French production, designed by Chéret, which included a vision of a placid Chinese lake. The

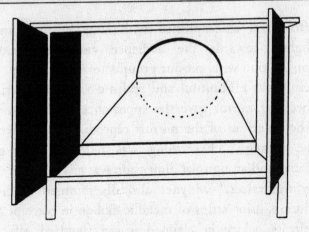

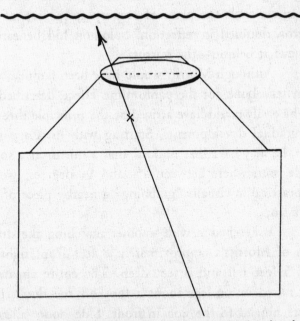

Top: A reconstruction of Morritt's Disappearing Donkey, based on Morritt's previous and subsequent illusions.
Bottom: An overhead view of the Donkey Cabinet, showing the sightlines which reflect off the mirror (at x) and to the scenery.

effect was accomplished with large mirrors, angled slightly towards the audience and positioned in conjunction with cut-out ground rows of scenery. The result was a beautiful and realistic view of water; the sheets of mirror gave the appearance of the lake and "the reflection of the mirrors reproduced and reversed the scenery.... Everything was reflected with great clarity and an unusual dimension was given to the stage by this effect." Moynet also diagrammed a similar illusion, using strips of metallic ribbon in place of glass mirrors, which he claimed was a standard effect in English pantomimes. For the Disappearing Donkey, the circle took the place of scenery at the top of the mirror, doubled in reflection. Solomon hid beneath—somewhat behind—the mirror.

Although Morritt would have been familiar with Moynet's book (or the pantomime effect described in it), he easily could have arrived at the principle through his gradual developments. Starting with his Cage illusion, he may have first noticed that a mirror at a softer angle, somewhere between 45- and 90-degrees, would be practical in visually "grabbing" a nearby piece of the backdrop.

I sketched a wide cabinet matching the drawings of Morritt's, approximately 8 feet from right to left, 5 feet tall and 3 feet deep. The entire apparatus was raised up on legs about a foot off the floor. Two doors hinged to the side in front. Side doors allowed the donkey to enter. The top hinged open, so it could be pushed open at the conclusion of the effect. The back was closed with a curtain.

According to this plan, the cabinet was virtually unprepared. Behind it was a shelf with an attached wedge-shaped container. It was designed something like a "lean-to," with a wide sloping roof. This roof was a trapezoidal sheet of mirror, the width of the cabinet at its front edge, narrowing to about 3 feet wide at its top edge. The reason for the trapezoid is that, protruding from the back of the cabinet, the container needed to be shaped to fall within audience sight-lines. The intention was that the audience only saw the mirrored roof of the load container, never the side walls which would betray its presence.

The mirror was hinged at its top rear edge, the 3-foot dimension. In this way it could be raised like a clamshell. (I added a narrow strip of wood, a sort of ground row at the back edge of the cabinet, which was also raised with the mirror.) When it was lowered, it closed over the shelf, trapping the donkey inside.

As before, Morritt provided a foreground object so the reflection of the mirror could be appreciated by the audience. In the case of the Donkey illusion, it was the fabric covered hoop, roughly 3 feet in diameter, which was placed against the top edge of the mirror. Actually, this hoop was clipped to the back of the load container, which seemed to suspend it in space. A single cord or two cords gave the impression that it was hanging.

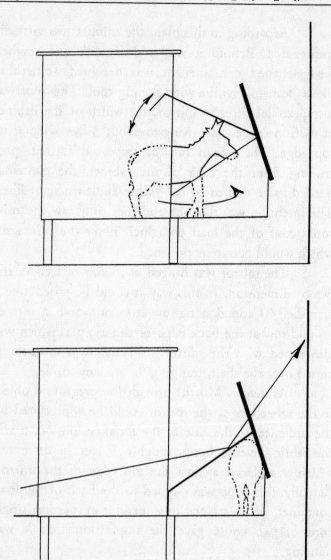

Top: A reconstruction of Morritt's Disappearing Donkey, a side view
showing the mirror hinged open and the donkey entering.
Bottom: The mirror closed in front of the donkey, showing the
sightlines which reflect off the mirror (at x) and to the scenery.

I made a scale model of the illusion to test those reflections. The angle of the glass was critical, shallower than 45-degrees. In this way the mirror "grabbed" a patch of backdrop some twelve to fifteen above the stage and reflected it as if it were directly behind the cabinet. As long as the backdrop was an even color or pattern, the slight discrepancy of the reflected angle could not be noticed. In a letter to Houdini, Morritt had written about the Disappearing Donkey, "there is no man could make this illusion without he actually measures it (sic), so no fear of imitation." There was nothing of the old "1 + 1" formula in his illusion, nothing so obvious.

•

The notion that Solomon was standing behind a mirror, hiding in plain sight, seemed logical. But, I realized that it was difficult drawing any conclusions until I actually met a donkey, measured it, inquired about its talent for hiding and its proclivity to perform. Although I've been on the back of a horse only a few times in my life, I happen to live near an equestrian center. I stopped by the local feed store to find the current installment of the horse journal, by chance an annual donkey and mule issue, and in a roundabout way found my way to Jerie Garbutt, several blocks away. Yes, she owned three donkeys, and invited me over to see them. There was Midget, a brown Sicilian donkey; Bridget, her doting mother; and Burrito, a suspicious and excitable jack (male) ass (donkey: both technical terms), with an apricot-gray colored coat.

I explained about Morritt, placed my model on the table in Jerie's backyard and showed her the sketches. Now, I told her, I wanted to measure some donkeys to see if it could work.

Jerie was able to provide commendable insight into a donkey's way of thinking. I asked if the donkey could have been trained to lay down or be lowered down. She thought not, explaining, "that would need to be a very, very trusting donkey." (I remembered the accounts of Morritt's neddy marching on-stage and promptly kicking over all the scenery.) She also gave me some practical advice. A characteristic twitch warns that a donkey is about to kick. It's better to throw yourself close to the donkey than try to step away; the kick, like a whip, has more power at the end of the arc. (Instinct made me run when I saw the twitch. I couldn't follow this advice.)

I stepped over the fence to take dimensions of Burrito, who wheezed and stomped through the experience, unhappy with the rattle of the tape measure. "But I don't exactly understand," Jerie said. "You're a magician and you want to perform this trick?" It was hard to make the exact point, that I was just interested in researching the history. After all, magicians perform, don't they? "Well," Jerie tried to accommodate my sliver of expertise, "I think we should do it. I've got the donkey. You build it, bring it here and I'll do the training."

I unwrapped a peppermint for Burrito (this was, Jerie showed me, the donkey's reward, and they prick up their ears at the sound of cellophane). I held the candy under his curling lips, then picked up my file of papers. I told Jerie I would think about the offer and thanked her.

"Well, I think you should do it," Alan Wakeling smiled, waving his fingers above the model to study the reflections. He quickly realized the principle, and that it would translate easily to the stage. "You've been working on it for years now. I mean, there's a donkey that lives around the corner from you. When are you going to have this chance again?"

For the record, donkeys are not stupid. Donkey owners will tell you that they're pretty smart. They are not as scattered or easily confused as horses. They are not, necessarily, stubborn. They are single-minded and relentless—which sometimes translates into stubbornness and sometimes is a virtue. Kim Gemmel, a donkey breeder from outside of Los Angeles, had cautioned me that the best way to move a donkey was by standing beside it and walking with it. "Don't stand in front and pull. They won't move. They'll lock up their legs and refuse to budge," Kim sensibly advised. In fact, a cute little donkey planting those four tiny hooves and standing firm, leaning, leaning, until gravity has been defied, is a sight which would have brought tears to Annie Abbott. But I knew from accounts that Morritt's donkey was pulled on-stage by the clown. The clown tugged and tugged, until the donkey froze and started kicking. Here was another insight into the presentation.

Poor Solomon was deliberately being cast as intractable and obstinate. It was part of the show!

•

I couldn't resist the opportunity to put a donkey through Charles Morritt's paces. Jerie and I set our sights on the November 1995 Conference on Magic History, six months away. It would be a sympathetic audience of collectors, historians and magicians, and a dozen people in the audience would be familiar with the problem and the Morritt story. Jerie nominated Midget for the role, her year-and-a-half old jennett (female) who was especially sociable and adventurous. I drew up plans for the apparatus, scaled to the donkeys I had met, and Willie Kennedy started on the prop. We decided to construct it in two pieces, the cabinet and the up-stage, trapezoidal load area which would contain the donkey.

The load space was a big, heavy construction. The mirror itself was quarter inch thick glass, eight feet wide at its down-stage edge and over three feet wide. Mounted on its steel and wood framework, it was well over one hundred pounds and would indeed have required "men under the stage" if they were hinging it up with ropes through pulleys in the top edge of the cabinet. In fact, this would have been the only efficient way of controlling the heavy mirror in conjunction with the donkey. Willie suggested using a modern alternative not available to Morritt, air cylinders like those which lift the hatchback of an automobile. This allowed one person inside the cabinet to easily lift or lower the mirror.

In some ways, the trapezoidal mirror remained accident prone. The mirror company cracked the first one while cutting it. Willie snapped the second mirror in transporting it. I had the most spectacular accident when the apparatus careened out of a truck on Riverside Drive in Burbank and shattered on the street. It took four mirrors until we got it right. Magicians cannot be superstitious about such accidents. Breaking mirrors is part of the job, even if this mirror seemed especially unlucky.

The circle was an essential part of the optical illusion. I had to decide how to disguise the edge of the mirror (which generally shows up as a dark line) against the light fabric of the hoop. Morritt may have used a clever solution, an additional thin strip of mirror on the leading edge, as he did in The Pillar Box. I used a piece of ribbon across the mirror edge, suggesting that the ribbon across the diameter of the hoop was part of the ribbon loop which suspended it.

As we began rehearsals, we discovered that the oversized cabinet would not fit through Jerie's gate, so we used only the mirrored load space in her paddock. Midget examined it and gradually grew bored with it. Every breakfast and dinner, she ate out of the contraption, soon coaxed into stepping inside, gradually finding the mirror closing on her as she ate. The first few times, thuds and stomps were quick to follow, but Midget soon succumbed to the charms of compressed alfalfa pellets. Once the mirror had closed against her side, the only sound was chewing.

I was very surprised at the practicality of it all, and how the odd geometry fit perfectly. A donkey occupied with dinner plants her legs firmly and lowers her head straight to the ground; in effect, she becomes a trapezoid which fits precisely behind the glass. The expected difficulty with a large glass mirror and a kicking donkey was never a problem in Morritt's arrangement. The mirror was lifted above the donkey before it entered, then lowered against it. The donkey only faced the back of the mirror, a wood surface. Besides, within such a tight confine, Jerie felt, Midget would be unable to make the proper "wind up" for a mighty kick. The size of the illusion was also right, eerily right. Built for a dog, for example, the cabinet would have been awkwardly small and low to the ground. (The shelf out the back becomes more visible as the legs of the cabinet grow taller.) Built for a horse, the apparatus would have been too large, requiring an impossibly heavy mirror and a reflection stretching so far overhead as to fall off the backdrop.

Midget's success encouraged us to connect both parts of the apparatus in my garage and attempt the entire routine. The early morning rehearsals, centered around Midget's meals, were suddenly difficult. The donkey didn't appreciate the ten minute walk to breakfast, was intimidated by the large cabinet and registered her displeasure with gravity-defying obstinacy. After several of these exhausting rehearsals, Jerie suggested moving Midget to my back yard, where she could live with the cabinet and gradually learn to step inside.

So, for the last two months of the enterprise, Midget became my donkey. She started every day with a precise 5:30 wake-up "feed me" call which, to my astonishment, had nothing to do with the rising sun. It was pitch black outside. The "song of the desert canary," my friend Bill Stout's term, is a loud, sudden gasp, then an ear-piercing screech like the amplified sound of a rusty hinge. My neighbors endured it with little complaint. ("Uh, is this donkey a permanent thing?") Gradually Midget learned to step inside the cabinet and returned to her familiar spot so that I could close the mirror. Then, with the mirror open again, I could use the temptation of peppermint to coax her back out of the cabinet. That jump, in fact any change of level, was an uncomfortable maneuver for the donkey, involving some forward and backward adjustments before the actual leap. But to her credit, Midget did learn to present the illusion without the benefit of a "second clown," that is, without an assistant inside maneuvering her into position. She learned the location of her food and resolutely entered the container so she could disappear.

Midget worked hard but was frustrated by rehearsals, the way a typical amateur fails to appreciate the call to show business. This sometimes manifested in a twitch and the promised kick. One fateful supper, which I delivered a bit later than she had wished, Midget managed to eat while delicately swinging around so she could kick me at the same time.

•

On November 11, 1995, I took the stage at the hotel ballroom as the rumbling overture came to a close.

I'd like to introduce the co-star of the show this evening. In all the world, there is only one...the one, the only, the Disappearing Donkey."

I gestured to the back of the audience. Jerie Garbutt has since told me how impressed she was with her donkey that night. Scratching at the ground, nibbling at plants and surveying the area suspiciously before the performance began, Midget seemed poised for trouble. But in the spotlight, to the cadence of a march, she pricked up her ears, looked straight ahead and made a sprightly entrance, leading Jerie down the aisle and to the stage. A friend of mine, an actor who was in the audience, later commented on what it's like to be in a large group of people when an animal walks in; how unexpected and strangely electrifying it feels. I knew only that Morritt had a good idea. Donkeys are funny. When Midget moved with determination it was funny. When she balked and resisted it was funny. A series of entreaties brought to her onto the stage.

It would be a very clever donkey indeed who could jump through this hoop without making a tear in the linen. I'm going to surround the cabinet using these two hoops, while you keep an eye on it. Take this hoop to the back of the cabinet and hang it on those loops of rib-bon....

The difficulty in any such reconstruction is restraint, in not bringing too much outside experience to the equation, or mistaking fashion for knowledge. For example, I reminded myself through the process that animals played different roles in magic than they do today. Unlike Siegfried and Roy, who have worked to tailor their magic to the animals and train them integrally for the secret, in 1912 the occasional donkey, horse or lion was merely a prop in the illusion. The magic occurred safely around them. Then again, the size of the apparatus—a big box to vanish a small donkey—was a product of the times. Today we would favor a tiny, form-fitting cabinet. How an illusion was seen, explained for the audience, and used through the routine, were all different than our current fashions.

There are also two doors in each side. That's the performer's entrance....

With the front doors closed, I stepped through the cabinet to demonstrate, secretly pulling open the mirrored fake in expectation of Midget. As it lifted it pushed up the hanging curtain in back, giving the donkey a clear path into her hiding place. In fact, this performance was not quite so uneventful. When she hopped into the cabinet, Midget failed to make the quick right turn to find her food and became confused. I guessed that it was best to step in after her and give a shove. She slid to the side, I quickly closed the mirror and came out again, slamming the side doors.

That's it. Open it up. She's gone!

It is difficult to calculate by what ingenuity a modern wizard could disguise such a secret. More than likely, it went unnoticed in the fits and starts which defined Charles Morritt's career. It was overlooked. After all, Devant himself explained the principle in his book. A patent spelled it out in detail. But Morritt's secret was cursed to be misunderstood because it was intuitive, not mathematical: not suited, like the last generations of magic, to line drawings. As a formula or diagram it fails, and for decades failed to convince. It needed to be massaged within cabinets and red plush drops, in train cars between Leeds and London, hammered from splinters of wood and pieces of mirror, then pushed and pulled, tweaked and adjusted. It was a matter of bits of looking glass, hidden under the pillow at night and arranged, rearranged, searching for something fresh.

Midget was gone. The cabinet was empty and the fabric circle hung suspended behind it, undisturbed. Quickly the front doors were shut and we secretly raised the mirror again, so that I could pull her from the cabinet for a final bow. Within seconds and with so little effort the Disappearing Donkey had suddenly reappeared, bolting from the cabinet: happy, blinking, oblivious to the applause and concentrating on the immediate goal, the peppermint which was held before her.

Notes

Many sources for this material were cited in the previous article. Thanks also to John Fisher and Pat Culliton for sharing valuable materials from their collections and important insights to Morritt's work. The Morritt letter to Houdini is in the collection of Stanley Palm.

The photo of Houdini with Hello Summer appeared in Doug Henning's *Houdini, His Legend and His Magic*, 1977. A staged portrait of Houdini with the paper hoop appeared in Milbourne Christopher's *Houdini, A Pictorial Life*, 1976.

M.J. Moynet's *L'Envers du Théatre* was published in Paris, 1875. I've taken English translation from the expanded Allan S. Jackson and M. Glen Wilson edition, *French Theatrical Production in the Nineteenth Century*, 1976.

The Magician Annual for 1908-9 reproduced a number of Morritt patents, including the Slat Mirror frame (issued to his wife Adelaide), the principle behind Oh! (with Nevil Maskelyne), and the Cage. The Pillar Box Mystery was explained as British patent 13,705 (with David Devant) issued in 1914. The Hello Summer principle was explained as British patent 9588, also issued in 1914. Curiously, a second claim, for a "conjuring table," was filed by Morritt on the date of this last patent, then later withdrawn. Possible reasons for the withdrawal are many, including a similarity between the inventions which confused the claim. Perhaps his conjuring table represented Ragtime Magic or Beauty and the Beast.

For the opportunity to perform the Disappearing Donkey, I am indebted to William Kennedy, Frankie Glass and my co-organizers of the Los Angeles Conference on Magic History: Mike Caveney, John Gaughan and Joan Lawton. Alan Wakeling watched from the front row. Jerie Garbutt wrote her own account of the performance in the Spring 1996 issue of *The Brayer*, published by the American Donkey and Mule Society. That evening, I had an opportunity to show the secret to several friends, including John Salisse and Elizabeth Warlock. One regret is that her father, Peter Warlock, was not able to see the reconstruction. He had seen the illusion as a boy, but remembered little towards its solution. Characteristically, his insights were still important, and Morritt's secrets were a favorite intrigue for Peter. After a long illness, he died just weeks after our Conference in 1995.

When I performed The Disappearing Donkey, Jay Marshall also examined the cabinet and asked, with his unique tone of mixed cynicism and intrigue, "How can you be so sure...?" I answered that I couldn't, but this was the only secret which accounts for the presentation and ties so tightly to Morritt's work. I believe that the explanations here and the gradual evolution of principles will explain my confidence.

However, I would be remiss to not mention Pat Page's valuable advice. Pat's experience in all phases of British magic is formidable. As I was attempting to reconstruct the secret, Pat suggested black art. He had no evidence, but believed that it was the only practical method for so large an animal. In fact, it is a very neat solution.

Imagine, for example, a shelf behind the cabinet which supported the donkey. A black velvet mask, like a theatrical flat, was hinged to hang in front of this, on the up-stage side of the cabinet. The white hoop would be placed on the shelf at the back; when the cabinet was opened a duplicate white disc, mounted permanently on the velvet flat, would be seen. This flat would be hinged up before the donkey entered. Once the animal was on the shelf, the flat would be lowered, giving the impression that the audience could still see through to the backdrop and the white hoop.

There are several sticking points; one is Devant's doors in back. It is difficult to arrange hinging doors around such a piece of masking scenery, although possible with the mirror. But the black art solution remains a real possibility. In this case, the illusion might have been the inspiration for Devant's 1913 illusion Biff, the vanishing motorcycle and rider, and tied far less to earlier Morritt illusions.

While I've made an effort to omit much of the technical information from this essay, reconstructions of other Morritt illusions may be in order, as there are family resemblances in all his magic. Goodbye Winter, the other illusion for Houdini, was the easiest to explain, the closest tie to Morritt's early mirror effects. Three tables, of decreasing size, were seen stacked on stage. The lady climbed a ladder to one side, slipped underneath the tablecloth covering the top table, then disappeared as the tablecloth was pulled away. The illusion was a descendant from Morritt's plank supported by four men. If the wedge of mirrors was concealed under the legs of the center table, it would conceal the lady after she passed through a trap door in the tabletop.

Most interesting was the note that the lady entered from a ladder to one side of the tables. This was typical of Morritt's tendency to tease a principle. With the wedge-shaped mirror arrangement, one side corner of the table can be approached by the performer without causing any reflections. The ladder was placed in a specific location.

The 1913 Pillar Box Mystery was also easily explained, as it had been the subject of a Morritt and Devant patent. Technically, Morritt was merely using the traditional "v-mirror" arrangement within a circular cabinet decorated as a post box. Morritt eliminated the need for a center post or masking over the vertical edge where the mirrors joined. By applying a narrow strip of mirror across the edges of the glass, a sort of triangle of thin mirror, the bare edges of the glass were disguised. If Morritt's goal was to use the exposed edges of a mirror on-stage, he was greatly enlarging the opportunities for such illusions.

An Elcock drawing of Morritt presenting The Panel, the production of a ghost from behind a thin panel of wood, portrays it atop the Beauty and the Beast octagonal table. This is the very best clue to this otherwise unknown illusion. S.H. Sharpe saw it performed as a boy and remembered very little about it. According to his 1985 book, *Conjurer's Optical Secrets*, he suspected that it may have been similar to Turkish Delight,

Ragtime Magic was next, a more elaborate production illusion. A long, thin table, waist high, extended right to left across the stage, with a narrow set of steps at the center. Four assistants in uniforms stood at regular intervals behind the table. Four framework boxes, spaced atop the table, were revolved and positioned with military precision by the assistants. Each was shown empty, then yards of fabric, the "rags" in question, were produced. Finally, the boxes were opened to show that each contained an assistant dressed as a boy scout.

The principle used in Beauty and the Beast, a wedge of mirrors behind a set of steps, with the apex on the up-stage side, is the sensible solution for Ragtime Magic. During the effect, the boxes were slid together, allowing the assistants to enter within the mirrors and move across to each box. In the case of Ragtime Magic, Morritt again teased his principle, accentuating its unusual points. Only the shallow, subtle angles of his mirrors would allow the four men to stand behind the table without causing stray reflections of legs.

Wodehouse Pittman's description of Tally Ho! (in the Davenport and Salisse book cited) was not very helpful and does not clearly suggest a principle. It seems logical that this horse production was, in some way, tied to similar Morritt effects. Tally Ho! was the production of a horse and rider, huntsman, "whipper-in" and hounds, according to the September 1915 *Magic Wand*.

Morritt's Black and White, a small square cupboard which slid forward and backward on a platform, and Chubb Safe Mystery seemed to suggest a connection to the early principle of the Mirror Tunnel. Black and White, in using a cloth background against the mirrors, also echoes the hoop in the Disappearing Donkey. The Mirror Tunnel was first seen in Walter Jeans' Silver Hat of 1912 and later in Selbit's Million Dollar Mystery, and could not have been far from Morritt's experiments with mirrors. (The 90 degree mirror, perpendicular to the backdrop, was the basic principle of the mirror tunnel and had been used in Morritt's Cage). From the various elements of his own illusions, Morritt should have reached the formula for the Mirror Tunnel. Finally and most tempting of all, Jeans was a resident of Leeds, the Yorkshire center of many of Morritt's enterprises. Did they meet and share their interests in such effects? What was happening up in Yorkshire in 1912?

Actually, it is interesting how the principle of the Disappearing Donkey anticipates and quickly leapfrogs over the Mirror Tunnel. Morritt's single mirror is set at the perfect angle to show it off, the circle behind it accentuates the open space with its reflection and provides a barrier behind the illusion. By contrast, Jeans' Mirror Tunnel is not appreciated by the audience directly in front of the apparatus. The audience at the sides, who can see the mirrors, understands that they can see behind the apparatus. Using a traditional mirror tunnel, the back of the apparatus cannot open, as this would reveal the connection to the fake. A discussion of the Jeans principle can be found in Peter Warlock's book, *Walter Jeans, Illusioneer*, published in 1986.

As for the various merits of these principles, I was able to use the elegant Vanishing Elephant principle again in an illusion of my own based on the comic situation of Sawing a Horse in Halves. This was presented on Lance Burton's 1996 NBC television special. The illusion surprised and deceived many magicians. Likewise, when it was shown at the Los Angeles Conference on Magic History, the Disappearing Donkey was a mystery to the audience. One otherwise astute magic reviewer offered that there were "no mirrors" used.

In 1997 at the Magic Collector's Weekend in Chicago, I presented the Morritt principles behind the donkey illusion in a lecture entitled, "Rediscovering Morritt."

About the Author

Jim Steinmeyer has invented many of the famous illusions used by leading magicians from Ricky Jay to Siegfried & Roy. He created David Copperfield's vanish of the Statue of Liberty and has also designed magic for six Broadway shows and many other productions, including *Mary Poppins*, currently playing in London's West End. He is the author of *Hiding the Elephant*, the *Los Angeles Times* bestseller, which Teller hailed as "a radiant celebration of the genius, glamour, and gargantuan egos of stage magic."

Steinmeyer has researched and rediscovered many great illusions of the past and has written numerous technical books on magic history and the techniques of magic. He lectures on these subjects and is a contributing editor to *Magic* magazine, the leading independent magazine for magicians.

In addition, Steinmeyer has served as consultant and producer for magic television specials in the United States and Great Britain, and was a writer and producer for the A&E network's four-hour history of the art, *The Story of Magic*. For several years, he served as a consultant and concept designer for Walt Disney Imagineering, developing theme park attractions for The Walt Disney Company.

Jim Steinmeyer lives in Los Angeles with his wife, Frankie Glass, an independent television producer. His next book for Carroll & Graf will be *The Gospel According to Charles Fort: Raining Fish, Talking Dogs, Dripping Blood, and the Writer Who Unhinged the Cosmos.*